What Ever Happened To Modernism?

Gabriel Josipovici is a novelist, literary theorist, critic and scholar. He was Professor of English at the University of Sussex, Weidenfeld Professor of Comparative Literature at Oxford, and is now research professor in the Graduate School of Humanities, Sussex. He has published three previous books with Yale, *The Book of God* (1988), *Touch* (1990) and *On Trust* (1999).

WHAT EVER HAPPENED TO MODERNISM?
GABRIEL JOSIPOVICI

YALE UNIVERSITY PRESS
NEW HAVEN AND LONDON

Copyright © 2010 Gabriel Josipovici

First printed in paperback 2011

For information about this and other Yale University Press publications, please contact:
U.S. Office: sales.press@yale.edu   www.yalebooks.com
Europe Office: sales @yaleup.co.uk   www.yaleup.co.uk

Set in Janson Text by IDSUK (DataConnection) Ltd
Printed in Great Britain by TJ International Ltd, Padstow, Cornwall

Library of Congress Cataloging-in-Publication Data
Josipovici, Gabriel, 1940–
    What ever happened to modernism?/Gabriel Josipovici.
        p. cm.
    ISBN 978–0–300–16577–7 (cl: alk. paper)
    1. Modernism (Literature)   I. Title.
    PN56.M54J67 2010
    809'.9112—dc22
                                                                        2010020776

A catalogue record for this book is available from the British Library.

ISBN 978–0–300–17800–5

10 9 8 7 6 5 4 3 2 1

To Gordon Crosse and John Mepham

'Nothing is granted me, everything has to be earned, not only the present and the future but the past too – something after all which perhaps every human being has inherited, this too must be earned, it is perhaps the hardest task.'

KAFKA, *Letters to Milena*

'Certain events would put me into a position in which I could not go on with the old language games any further. In which I was torn away from the sureness of the game.'

WITTGENSTEIN, *On Certainty*

'Do you mean to say the story is finished?' said Don Quixote.
    'As finished as my mother,' said Sancho.

MIGUEL DE CERVANTES, *Don Quixote*

Contents

Figures

Preface

The first extra-curricular lecture I attended at Oxford was an address given to the Literary Society by Lord David Cecil on the topic of 'The English Novel Today'. It was the autumn of 1958. I had just spent a happy year between school and university getting to know London, the first city I had ever lived in, and using the wonderful Putney and Wandsworth public libraries to read my way through as much of world literature as I could, starting with the writers I had discovered in my last years at school, Eliot, Donne and Kafka, and going on to Tolstoy and Dostoevsky, Proust and Mann. Now I hurried to Lord David's lecture, eager to discover who were the English writers currently at work who were, so to speak, following in those footsteps.

I remember nothing about the lecture except that it was full to the rafters, suggesting that I was not the only one who had come eager to learn, but I did come away with a list of names: Anthony Powell, Angus Wilson and, said Lord David, a young writer to watch, Iris Murdoch. However, when I borrowed their work from the library I was disappointed to find that they seemed to have nothing whatsoever in common with the writers I had been reading. They told entertaining stories wittily or darkly or with sensationalist panache, and they obviously wrote well, but theirs were not novels which touched me to the core of my being, as had those of Kafka and Proust. Since I had plenty to do learning Anglo-Saxon and reading the authors on the syllabus, plus the still unread works of Thomas Mann, I did not stop to ask myself why this should be so and whether the fault lay with me or with them, but simply let the matter drop.

Three years later, as a graduate student, I felt that the time had come for me to take a new look at 'the English novel today'. I had discovered Borges, first in the pages of *Encounter* and then in French translation on the shelves of the old Parker's, and I had just been reading all the books of Claude Simon I could lay my hands on, having been alerted to him by a glowing review by Philip Toynbee in the *Observer* of his most recent novel, *L'Herbe*, with its wonderful epigraph from Pasternak: 'No-one makes history, we do not see it, any more than we see the grass grow.' Alain Robbe-Grillet had also recently visited Oxford as a guest of the Maison Française, as a result of which I had read *Le Voyeur* and was still reeling under the impact. It was clear that out there in Argentina and France and no doubt in lots of other countries there *were* writers whose work belonged to the same world as that of Proust and Kafka and Eliot. It was time to take another look at their English counterparts and see if I had misjudged them. To my disappointment I quickly discovered that whatever it was that had put me off the first time round had not gone away. They still said nothing to me, still seemed to be 'English' in a way Borges and Simon and Robbe-Grillet were not Argentinian or French, still seemed to belong to a different and inferior world to that of Proust and the others.

In the course of the following decades, in the intervals between writing my own novels and plays and my teaching duties, I sometimes turned to writing about those authors who meant much to me, dead ones like Kafka and Proust, and living ones like Borges, Bellow, Georges Perec and Aharon Appelfeld. There were only two English authors in this personal pantheon: William Golding, whose best work, I felt, had been done before the mid-1960s, and Muriel Spark, who had left England for New York and then Italy. In my innocence I imagined that by writing about these authors I would not only make people see what they were really up to, but could also help them grasp the nature and implications of that Modernism of which I felt they formed a part. Instead of which I found that English culture was actually growing steadily *less* interested in or aware of these issues. The *Encounter*s and the Philip Toynbees, magazines and critics with a European sensibility, whose imaginative borders stretched beyond Victorian and post-war England, had long gone and not been replaced, and the new lead critics of the Sunday papers and cultural weeklies, though many of them would have been horrified to know it, held fundamentally the same views as had Lord David Cecil in the late 1950s. The lending libraries, too, which had been one of the glories of the Britain on whose shores I had landed in 1956, had slowly withered and, in some cases, died. I read all the new writers these critics recommended, for one is always looking for something exciting and fulfilling to read, but I invariably came away with the same sense of disappointment as I had had when seeking to follow up Lord David's recommendations. Occasionally I wondered why my own feelings and those of the reviewers and critics were so much at odds, wondered, indeed, who was right, me or the entire establishment. I didn't think I was mad (though of course the mad rarely do), and I did occasionally meet people who shared my tastes, so how was this anomaly to be explained?

This little book is an attempt to answer that question. It has not been easy to write. For reasons I discuss in the final chapter, a book of this kind must inevitably be personal, but that does not mean that it should be merely subjective: I wish to persuade my reader, not simply air my opinions. Yet it is difficult to walk the thin line between didacticism and rant, and between giving too much information and too little. In writing about a single author or work such issues do not arise: one focuses on the object and everything has to be directed towards the one aim of bringing out into the open what one thinks makes that author or work important and meaningful. But what should be the focus of a book like the present one? At times it seems to be nothing less than life itself, at others a problem of syntax. That is why there are so many excellent books on individual Modernists, such as Hugh Kenner's *The Invisible Poet* (on Eliot), Erich Heller's *The Ironic German* (on Mann), Deleuze and Guattari's *Pour une littérature mineure* (on Kafka), and hardly any good books, so far as I am aware, on Modernism. The reason is that the authors of such books either reduce everything to a lowest common denominator or seem hopelessly biased and partisan. I have learned much, though, from Marthe Robert's *L'Ancien et le nouveau*, a study of the 'newness' of *Don Quixote* and Kafka's *The Castle*, from Geoffrey Hartman's early *The Unmediated Vision*, and from the essays of Erich Heller, Maurice Blanchot and Roland Barthes. I have also found, while writing this book, that art historians seem at present to be much more alive to the issues I am interested in (Modernism is still perceived as an issue in art criticism) than literary critics, and I have understood much about the topic from reading Rosalind Krauss's *The Picasso Papers* and T.J. Clark's *Farewell to an Idea*.

In the end, though, this is a personal book, an attempt, fifty years on, to clarify the unease I felt in those early days in Oxford, which has only grown in the intervening years. I hope, however, that it says something not just about myself but about our world, about artists, and about art.

Lewes, 1 October 2009

1

My Whole Body Puts Me On My Guard Against Each Word

In 1864 Mallarmé, aged twenty-three, wrote to his friend Henri Cazalis: 'I feel I'm collapsing in on myself day by day, each day discouragement overwhelms me, and the lethargy is killing me. When I emerge from this I'll be stupefied, nullified (. . . *Chaque jour le découragement me domine, je meurs de torpeur. Je'sortirai de là abruti, annulé*).' Shortly after this Mallarmé began work on a verse tragedy, *Hérodiade*, but was soon struck down by another bout of poetic impotence:

> On top of that I am disgusted by my self; I step back from the mirror, seeing my face worn out and without any life in it, and cry when I feel myself to be empty and cannot put pen to the implacably white paper. To be an old man and finished at twenty-three, when all those we love live in the midst of light and flowers, at the age of the creation of masterpieces! [. . . *Etre un vieillard, fini, à vingt-trois ans, alors que tous ceux qu'on aime vivent dans la lumière et les fleurs, à l'âge des chefs-d'oeuvre!*]

Nearly forty years later, in 1901, the young Austrian poet, Hugo von Hofmannsthal, wrote a strange little work in which he tried to explain to himself and the world why he had found himself unable to go on with his brilliant career as a poet. The work takes the form of a letter purportedly written by Lord Chandos, a young country gentleman of the Elizabethan period, to his older friend, the statesman and philosopher Francis Bacon. 'My condition is this', he writes:

> I have quite lost the faculty to think or speak on any subject in a coherent fashion. To begin with, it gradually became impossible

for me to converse on any higher or general subject, and to use those words which all men use constantly and unhesitatingly. I felt inexplicably loath even to say 'Mind' or 'Soul' or 'Body'.

Gradually, however, the whole of language became infected. He seemed no longer able to grasp things 'through the simplifying regard of habit', as other people seemed to do:

> Everything fell into pieces in front of me, the pieces into more pieces, and nothing could be contained in a single concept any more. Individual words swam around me; they melted into eyes, which stared at me, and which I had to stare back at; they are like whirlpools, it gives me vertigo to look down at them, they turn without cease, and transport you into nothingness.

He tries to rescue himself from this plight by turning to the Ancients, to Seneca and Cicero in particular:

> I hoped to cure myself with that harmony of limited and orderly concepts. But I was unable to reach them. Their concepts I could well understand: rising before me like majestic fountains with golden balls ... I could float around them and see how they played together; but they were only concerned with each other, and the deepest, most individual part of my thought was excluded from their dance. In their company, I was overcome by a feeling of terrible solitude; I felt like someone who had been locked into a garden full of eyeless statues.

Since then, his 'existence has been one that, I fear, you will hardly be able to comprehend, so devoid of mind and thought is it'. Outwardly he seems no different from those around him, but inwardly he is a changed man. Yet, he explains to the chancellor, this is an existence not entirely devoid of good moments, though these take a form which it is impossible to explain to another:

> For it is something that has never been named and that it is probably impossible to name, which manifests itself to me at such moments, taking some object from my everyday surroundings, and filling it like a vessel with an overflowing torrent of higher

life ... A watering-can, a harrow left abandoned in a field, a dog in the sun, a poor churchyard, a cripple, a small farmhouse, any one of these can become a vessel for my revelation.

Apart from these strange occurrences, though, 'which, by the way,' he adds, 'I can hardly say whether they should be called physical or spiritual,' 'I lead a life of almost unbelievable emptiness', rendered all the more painful by the knowledge

that in the next year, and the year hereafter, and in all the years of my life I shall write no English and no Latin book: and this for a reason whose – to me – distressing strangeness I leave it to your boundless intellectual superiority to place with an undazzled vision there where it belongs in the array of physical manifestations that are harmoniously spread out before you: namely, because the language in which it might perhaps have been given to me not only to write, but also to think, is neither Latin nor English, nor Italian nor Spanish, but a language of which I do not know even one word, a language in which dumb things speak to me, and in which I may once, in my grave, have to account for myself before an unknown judge.

Ten years after the writing of 'The Letter of Lord Chandos', in another major city of the soon-to-disappear Austro-Hungarian Empire, Prague, we find the twenty-seven-year-old Franz Kafka confiding to his diary an experience not dissimilar to that of Hofmannsthal's Elizabethan gentleman. While in his office, dictating a report,

towards the end, where a climax was intended, I got stuck and could do nothing but look at Fraülein K, the typist, who, in her usual way, became especially lively, moved her chair about, coughed, tapped on the table ... Finally I have the word 'stigmatize' and the appropriate sentence, but still hold it all in my mouth with disgust and a sense of shame as though it were raw meat, cut out of me [... *Endlich habe ich das Wort 'brandmarken' und den dazu gehörigen Satz, halte aber noch im Mund mit einem Ekel and Schamgefühl, wie wenn es rohes Fleisch, aus mir geschnittenes Fleisch wäre*].

A year earlier he had written to his closest friend, Max Brod, with whom he had recently undertaken a trip to Paris:

> I can't write. I haven't written a single line that I can accept, instead I have crossed out all I have written – there wasn't much – since my return from Paris. My whole body puts me on my guard against each word; each word, even before letting itself be put down, has to look round on every side; the phrases positively fall apart in my hands, I see what they are like inside and then I have to stop quickly.

Twelve years later, with most of what we consider to be his greatest work (the defining work, Auden believed, of the twentieth century) behind him, Kafka sends another letter to Brod, which makes it clear that those early remarks are not the usual grumbles of a budding artist frustrated at not being able to find his voice, but something more unusual and much more troubling:

> During last night's insomnia, as these thoughts came and went between my aching temples, I realised once again, what I had almost forgotten in this recent period of relative calm, that I tread a terribly tenuous, indeed almost non-existent soil spread over a pit full of shadows, whence the powers of darkness emerge at will to destroy my life . . . Literature helps me to live, but wouldn't it be truer to say that it furthers this sort of life? Which of course doesn't imply that my life is any better when I don't write. On the contrary, then it's much worse, quite unbearable, and with no possible remedy other than madness.

Some forty years on again and we find Samuel Beckett, an Irishman long resident in Paris, publishing, in French, a series of dialogues on painters and painting with the art critic and son-in-law of Matisse, Georges Duthuit. In the first of these, on Tal-Coat, the Dutch painter so admired by Wallace Stevens as well as himself, he says: 'I speak of an art . . . weary of puny exploits, weary of pretending to be able, of being able, of doing a little better the same old thing, of going a little further along a dreary road.' What would you put in its place? asks a puzzled Duthuit. 'The expression that there is nothing to express,' responds

Beckett, 'nothing with which to express, nothing from which to express, no power to express, no desire to express, together with the obligation to express.'

I could go on with my examples. I could quote from Melville's *Bartleby* and from Mann's *Doktor Faustus*, from Henry James's *Notebooks* and from Paul Celan's speech on receiving the Büchner Prize; I could turn to musicians and painters and quote from the letters of Schoenberg and the interviews Francis Bacon gave to David Sylvester, from Giacometti's comments to James Lord and Geörgy Kurtág's account of his Paris crisis in the mid-1950s. But there would be no point. Let these four examples stand for a century of pain, anxiety and despair on the part of writers, painters and composers, and let their words stand for what has been called the Crisis of Modernism.

How are we to respond to this? One way is to ignore it altogether, as does Peter Gay in his recent *Modernism: The Lure of Heresy*. This dreadful book exemplifies everything that is wrong with positivist history: lacking any questions to put to the past it opts for a mere account of 'what happened', and, needing somehow to organise the mass of material, comes up with the theory (though that is too kind to it) that Modernism consisted of two strands – a desire to shock the bourgeoisie and a desire to express subjectivity. The first allows Gay to concentrate (with relief, one feels) on such public events as the trials of Flaubert and Baudelaire for obscenity; the second becomes a mantra he can trot out whenever he is faced by a Modernist work. Thus we are told that 'modernist painters . . . exhibit their innermost being' and that 'the modernist novel is an exercise in subjectivity'. The trouble with the first is that it focuses on a superficial aspect of Modernism, with the second that it is so vague as to be meaningless when it is not at odds with the observable facts, as, for example, when Gay wryly notes that Kafka does not seem to be particularly interested in subjectivity. Though Gay's book is especially bad, it is typical of those studies of the subject which seek to ignore that there was a crisis at all and try merely to describe 'what happened' between 1880 and 1940, as they would try to describe 'what happened' at any other period.

More interesting, if scarcely more illuminating, are those responses which note the symptoms of a crisis only to dismiss them with various degrees of disdain or condescension. One example of this was typified for me by a lecture I heard given by the first professor of philosophy at the University of Sussex, Patrick Corbett. Corbett was a huge man, and, as he spoke, he prowled round the lectern, kicking at the wainscoting and the floor. The lecture went something like this: 'Kierkegaard! Hunh! (*kick*) Nietzsche! Hunh! (*kick*) Dostoevsky! Hunh! (*kick*) Baudelaire! Hunh! (*kick*) Sartre! Hunh! (*kick*) Nothing that a good walk on the Downs wouldn't have put right!' In other words, these effete ninnies were all suffering from oversensitivity mingled with self-regard; what they had to say was the result of their cosseted upbringing and a sharp kick up the backside was all that was needed to bring them to their senses. This of course has always been the response of the majority of Englishmen to Modernist artists and thinkers. In December 1945 Evelyn Waugh wrote a letter to *The Times*, commenting on an exhibition of Picasso and Matisse which had just opened at the Victoria and Albert Museum. Waugh's wit and his mastery of the English language cannot hide the rage he feels when, with the war just won at enormous sacrifice, he and his fellow-countrymen are subjected to such continental posturing:

> Señor Picasso's painting cannot be intelligently discussed in the terms used of the civilised masters . . . The large number of otherwise cultured and intelligent people who fall victim to Señor Picasso are not posers. They are genuinely 'sent'. It may seem preposterous to those of us who are immune, but the process is apparently harmless. They emerge from their ecstasy as cultured and intelligent as ever. We may even envy them their experience. But do not let us confuse it with the sober and elevating happiness which we derive from the great masters.

Though the names may have changed, and Picasso is now generally accepted, this is still the view of a large section of the British public today, given the courage to voice their view by the likes of Philip Larkin and Kingsley Amis, whose epistolary exchanges ('all these cheerless craps between 1900 and 1930 – Ginny Woolf and Dai Lawrence and Morgy Forster') are exactly on a par with Waugh's letter and Corbett's lecture.

A more sophisticated critique of Modernism is the Marxist one I heard put forward by another Sussex professor, Eduard Goldstücker, a charming and cultivated man who had fled Czechoslovakia when the Russian tanks rolled into Prague in 1968, but who had, before that, as rector of Charles University, been responsible for making Kafka acceptable inside the Soviet bloc. He maintained that, intelligent and perceptive as writers like Kierkegaard and Kafka were, what they really tell us is that the bourgeoisie was in crisis and that what they took to be personal and artistic problems were in fact social ones, and that once these were resolved, as they one day would be, we would look back on them and their complaints as historical curiosities.

Finally, there is a completely different kind of response which we might label the post-Modern. This takes the form of saying that we are all infinitely flexible, that we can all choose our traditions as and where we like, so that there is no need to get into a state about a crisis in one tradition, we simply need to let it go and jump onto another train, as it were. The anxiety, not to say obsession, evinced by the Modernists betrays, the post-Modernist suggests, an unwarranted belief in Truth and Self. There are, however, he argues, many truths and many selves, and what the angst expressed by these writers shows is how much they were still in thrall to now outdated notions which had long been dear to Western thought but which we have now thankfully laid to rest.

None of the charges put forward by the last three groups of critics is entirely silly. One can easily lose patience with Kafka's masochism and his self-centredness, with Picasso's egotism and Beckett's elegant, almost mannered, expressions of despair. Reading Waugh taking pot shots at Picasso and Wittgenstein, or Larkin and Amis laughing at Virginia Woolf and E.M. Forster, is refreshing – we don't, after all, want to worship them, or any artist. But unfortunately what we get is not simply a criticism of what these artists were like as human beings or of the adulation they evoked in this or that coterie; it slips all too easily into a response to their work, and one can't help feeling that Larkin and Amis are rather like little boys overawed at a grown-up party and determined to show they aren't by being rude to the guests. (Waugh is much grander and more sure of himself; his philistinism exudes the confidence of a long tradition of smoking-room suspicion of continental poseurs.)

As for Goldstücker, there is a point to his view that this is a social as much as an artistic crisis. It is not a crisis, though, that has an obvious solution, whether social or artistic. The post-Modernist too puts his finger on a real problem: Modernists do occasionally give the impression that they are fighting old battles with inadequate tools. But the best explorations of the issue, whether by the artists themselves, or by such critics as Maurice Blanchot, Walter Benjamin or Erich Heller, are undertaken with full awareness of these pitfalls, while at the same time denying that we can simply choose our traditions as and where we want them.

The main point to make about all three charges, however, is that the travails of the Modernists are so intimately bound up with their achievements that it feels simply impertinent to condescend to them, as all these responses do, as though *we* understood what was wrong with *them* and could set them right with a remark or two. They laid their lives on the line, after all, and though we might feel that they were misguided we should think twice before presuming to tell them they were wrong.

In order to understand that there are good reasons for the difficulties they encountered in getting their work not just published but written, and that these difficulties are part and parcel of what makes them rewarding to read, we have to try and see Modernism not from without, as Gay, Corbett, Goldstücker and the post-Modernist choose to see it, but from within. That is the task of this book.

I

THE DISENCHANTMENT OF THE WORLD

2

The Oracles Are Silent

When does Modernism begin? That seems an innocent enough question, but it is actually the source of many of the problems we have in coming to terms with it. Since the passages I quoted in the last chapter from Mallarmé, Hofmannsthal, Kafka and Beckett all fall between the years 1850 and 1950 the temptation is strong to date Modernism in that hundred-year period. This is certainly when it flourished and when its manifestations were so prevalent that no-one could ignore it. The danger in seeing it like that, though, is that Modernism is thereby turned into a style, like Mannerism or Impressionism, and into a period of art history, like the Augustan or the Victorian age, and therefore as something that can be clearly defined and is safely behind us. I, on the other hand, want to argue that Modernism needs to be understood in a completely different way, as the coming into awareness by art of its precarious status and responsibilities, and therefore as something that will, from now on, always be with us. Seen in this way, Modernism, I would suggest, becomes a response by artists to that 'disenchantment of the world' to which cultural historians have long been drawing our attention.

That phrase was given currency by the sociologist Max Weber in the early years of the twentieth century. In *The Protestant Ethic and the Spirit of Capitalism* (1904) and in later essays, he argued that the Reformation was part of a historical process 'the disenchantment of the world' (*die Entzauberung der Welt*), whereby the sacramental religion of the Middle Ages was transformed into a transcendental and intellectualised religion, which led to the disappearance of the numinous from everyday life. In England this shift has mainly been seen as what the authors of *1066 and All*

That would have called a Good Thing, since it led us from an era of superstition to our modern era of common sense and scientific understanding, from the darkness of the Middle Ages to the light of the Enlightenment. A monument of English Renaissance history, Keith Thomas's *Religion and the Decline of Magic* (1971) is a fine example of this attitude. 'Despite the studiously agnostic, anthropological spirit in which he conducted his inquiry', a recent historian has written about this, 'he . . . subscribed implicitly to the view that the Reformation helped to emancipate the English populace from a "superstitious" understanding of the world around them, from assumptions which, he wrote in the foreword, were now "rightly disdained by intelligent persons".' And, despite the splendid work of writers such as Eamon Duffy, who for over twenty years has been attempting to rescue late medieval culture from the contempt of (largely Protestant) historians, this view has remained the common one in the English-speaking world.

This is not surprising, since it feeds into another powerful myth, that of the Renaissance as the triumph of the individual after centuries of subservience to authority and tradition, centuries of being bound to the yoke of religion and superstition. Both these myths, the myth of light coming out of darkness and the myth of the emancipation of the individual, were of course first propagated by Protestants and Humanists themselves, and both have been shown to be, if not downright lies, at least only one side of the story, but the assumptions behind them live on in our culture as obvious truths, repeated every time religion is criticised as mere superstition or when a caption to a painting in a gallery draws attention to the lifelikeness of what is being depicted, implying that 'lifelikeness', that Renaissance ideal, is what all art aspires to.

Things are rather different in the German tradition. There cultural analysts such as Erich Heller, Hans-Georg Gadamer and Hans Blumenberg have sought to bring out what has got lost as well as what has been gained by the transition from older ways of thinking to modernity. This is perhaps not surprising when we remember that the phrase, 'the disenchantment of the world' is originally Schiller's, and that all Schiller's mature critical writing is an attempt to come to terms with what he eloquently describes as the disappearance of a glorious earlier age (he is thinking, in somewhat idealised terms, of the Greeks), an age in which man was simply a part of the world, while now he stands outside, looking in, aware only of what he has lost. The feeling is ubiquitous among the Romantics, especially the German Romantics; perhaps its most eloquent expression is to be found in Hegel's *Phenomenology of Spirit* (1807), where the philosopher explores what he calls 'the unhappy consciousness'. 'Trust in the eternal laws of the gods has vanished', he writes,

> and the Oracles, which pronounced on particular questions, are dumb. The statues are now only stones from which the living soul has flown, just as the hymns are words from which belief has gone. The tables of the gods provide no spiritual food and drink, and in his games and festivals man no longer recovers the joyful consciousness of his unity with the divine. The works of the Muse now lack the power of the Spirit, for the Spirit has gained its certainty of itself from the crushing of gods and men. They have become what they are for us now – beautiful fruit already picked from the tree, which a friendly Fate has offered us, as a girl might set the fruit before us. It cannot give us the actual life in which they existed, not the tree that bore them, nor the earth and the elements which constituted their substance, not the climate which gave them their peculiar character nor the cycle of the changing seasons that governed the process of their growth. So fate does not restore their world to us along with the works of antique Art, it gives not the spring and summer of the ethical life in which they blossomed and ripened, but only the veiled recollection of that actual world.

Critics and cultural historians are sharply divided into those who find remarks of this kind illuminating and those who think them either arrant nonsense or the expression of a purely private anxiety. But the position you adopt does not depend simply on faith. Those, including myself, who find remarks like Hegel's or Schiller's illuminating, do so in part because they help us to recognise that this sense of somehow having arrived too late, of having lost for ever something that was once a common possession, is a, if not *the*, key Romantic concern.

But is this not merely setting back the onset of Modernism by half a century? If you wish to see 'the disenchantment of the world' as a key ingredient in Modernism, a critic of this line of thought might argue, is not what you are doing merely eliding Modernism and Romanticism? To pose these questions is once again to misunderstand what is at issue. It is to deny that Hegel's present tense, his insistent 'now . . . now . . . now . . .', is still the present tense for us – i.e., that we still live in the world Hegel so movingly describes. That, I suspect, is what divides English and continental philosophy, and that is the task of this book: to try to bring home to readers the sense in which Hegel's present tense is still present for us.

There is a further point. To see Modernism as beginning in 1800 rather than 1850 is short-sighted in another way. T.S. Eliot famously located a 'dissociation of sensibility' in the mid-seventeenth century, while cultural critics like Heller and Blumenberg, perhaps taking their cue from Weber, would take it back even further, to the early sixteenth century and the coming of Protestantism. Heller even, and only half in jest, once pointed to a moment in 1529 when, he said, the problems of modern poetry began. The occasion was a disputation in the ducal castle in Marburg between Martin Luther and Huldrych Zwingli, who had been brought together by Philip of Hesse in an attempt to heal the splits that were beginning to show in the ranks of the Reformers less than a dozen years after Luther had nailed his theses to the Castle Church doors in Wittenberg and unwittingly set the Reformation in train. The subject of dispute was the nature of the eucharist: were the bread and wine administered by the priest, as Luther, in this still a man of the Middle Ages, insisted, really the body and blood of Christ, or were they, as the Humanist Zwingli maintained, merely symbolic? Zwingli could not believe that Luther, who had challenged the authority of pope and councils and denounced pilgrimages and purgatory as superstitious practices designed to make money for the Church, could really believe that Christ, who sat in heaven on the right hand of God, could also be present in the wine and bread used by priests all over Christendom every day of the year. But Luther, for his part, clung to his belief: a cultured man like Zwingli might laugh, but he knew in his soul that the mystery of the eucharist was real, that the ritual was not designed merely to bring to the memory of the participant that first sacrifice of Christ; it was actually to partake, in some way, in that sacrifice.

The parties could not agree and could not even devise a face-saving formula. As Heller points out, the dispute was not even new, since theologians had been arguing about the precise nature of transubstantiation for centuries. But it had taken on a new importance and after the Marburg disputation there was no going back, for theology or for Western man. 'Of course,' says Heller,

I do not confuse a theological controversy with an exercise in aesthetic theory. But I do suggest that at the end of a period that we rather vaguely call the Middle Ages there occurred a radical change in man's idea of reality, in that complex fabric of unconsciously held convictions about what is real and what is not. This was a revolution comparable to that earlier one which Nietzsche called the victory of the Socratic mind over the spirit of Dionysian tragedy. And indeed both victories saddled us with the unending bother of aesthetic philosophy.

The Marburg debate brings out the fact that the Protestant revolution was not one thing which in a single moment changed the face of European politics, religion and thought. The world did not become disenchanted overnight. It was, rather, the coming out into the open of doubts and confusions that had not, until then, found a clear voice. As Luther's stance at Marburg suggests, the 'medieval' and the 'modern' were to coexist for a long while yet. But the fabric of thought was changing. Take the Reformers' polemics against Purgatory. The idea that there was a middle state 'in which', as a recent historian has put it, 'those whom God loved would have a chance to perfect the hard slog towards holiness that they had begun so imperfectly in their brief earthly life' was nowhere to be found in the Bible, and by the fifteenth century, when rich nobles could set up chantry chapels and hire priests to sing daily masses in perpetuity to help speed them through Purgatory as quickly as possible, the whole doctrine had begun, to some, to seem meaningless and mechanical. But the idea of men on earth, by their devotions, helping those who had died and earning themselves benefit from their labours in the eyes of God was one which would have been understood by most so-called primitive peoples, for it is based on the belief that there is a profound link between groups of human beings and between the living and the dead. In the *Choephori* of Aeschylus, the second play of his trilogy about the House of Agamemnon, known as the *Oresteia*, Agamemnon's two surviving children, Electra and Orestes, egged on by the chorus, pray at the tomb of their murdered father for him to help them avenge his fate on the culprit, their mother. At the climax of this extraordinary scene Orestes cries out to his father:

> And do not wipe out this Pelopid seed; for then [i.e. if you do suffer them to be wiped out], even though dead, you will not have perished. For to a dead man his children are the fame that preserves him; like corks they bear the net up, keeping safe the spun flax that stretches up from the depths.
>
> (ll.503–7, tr. Alan H. Somerstein)

For Aeschylus, the unit is not the individual but the family, the House, here defined by reference to the first ancestor, Pelops. Man by himself is nothing; only the family, the House, gives meaning to his life. Just as for Aristotle a little later, man is less than human if he is not functioning within a unit larger than himself, the *polis* or city state. When in the sixteenth century Reformers everywhere rounded on the doctrine of Purgatory, they were, like Zwingli in his argument with Luther, absolutely right in their own eyes; what they were attacking *was* nonsense, it *was* a form of superstition. But what they could not see was that their new clear-sightedness was the result of the disappearance of an older way of looking at things which was itself dependent on older forms of social organisation. In the nineteenth century scholars were in no doubt at all that the Reformers were right every time, that they were finally waking up to the absurdities of superstition. In the twentieth century, though voices like those of Keith Thomas were still in the majority, there were some who were no longer quite so sure. And there were some, like Heller, who were prepared to see what had got lost in the transition as well as what had been gained, who would even see the transition as tragic. That certainly, is the stance of Thomas Mann, in the most eloquent artistic exploration of the issue, his last major novel, *Doctor Faustus*.

Adrian Leverkühn, the novel's composer-hero, is profoundly aware, as his friend and biographer Serenus Zeitblom is not, of the crisis that has engulfed art since the sixteenth century; Leverkühn's entire intellectual and artistic life is built out of a deep awareness of the contrast between the 'age of cult' and the 'age of the individual', that is, between the Middle Ages and what followed. Practically every page of this long novel has some remarkable critical insight based on that distinction, so, rather than following the well-trodden paths and examining again what is said in a general and philosophical way in the central chapters of the book, let me turn to a passage close to the end, where Mann/Zeitblom is attempting to describe the effect of Leverkühn's last great work, '*The Lamentation of Doctor Faustus*':

> The *Lamentation*, that is – and what we have here is an abiding, inexhaustibly accentuated lament of the most painfully Eccehomo kind – the Lamentation is expression itself; one may state boldly that all expressivism is really lament; just as music, so soon as it is conscious of itself as expression at the beginning of its modern history, becomes lament and '*lasciatemi morire*' [*die Klage ist der Ausdruck selbst, man kann kühnlich sagen, dass aller Ausdruck eigentlich Klage ist, wie denn die Musik, sobald sie sich als Ausdruck begreift, am Beginn ihrer modernen Geschichte, zur Klage wird und zum 'Lasciatemi morire'*], the lament of Ariadne, to the softly echoing plaintive song of the nymphs. It does not lack significance that the Faust cantata is stylistically so strongly and unmistakably linked with the seventeenth century and Monteverdi, whose music – again not without significance – favoured the echo-effect, sometimes to the point of being a mannerism. The echo, the giving back of the human voice as nature-sound, and the revelation of it *as* nature-sound, is essentially a lament: Nature's melancholy 'Alas!' in view of man, her effort to utter his solitary state. Conversely, the lament of the nymphs on its side is related to the echo. In Leverkühn's last and loftiest creation, echo, a favourite device of the baroque, is employed with unspeakably mournful effect.

Thus, says Mann, when the choral music of the Middle Ages, the music of community, gives way in the Renaissance to opera, with its celebration of the individual, this is, for music, not entirely a matter for rejoicing. It is no coincidence that Monteverdi's first and greatest opera, *Orfeo* (1607, usually seen as the first opera *tout court*), should take as its subject one of the ancient world's main legends of irreparable loss, a legend that has haunted modern artists from Rilke to Birtwistle as it haunted the Renaisssance. Like Dowland's almost contemporary *Lachrymae* (1605), recently so beautifully touched into life by Birtwistle in his *Semper Dowland, Semper Dolens*, and, like countless Renaissance sonnets, it is specifically about the loss of a beloved woman, but the reason it has exerted such a hold is clearly that, like Monteverdi's 'Ariadne's Lament', it is about some deeper, more primal and all-encompassing loss. The Middle Ages, of course, had their fair share of poems and songs about the loss of a loved one, but these songs have a kind of upswing and energy that belies their subject-matter. What is so extraordinary about 'Ariadne's Lament' and Dowland's *Lachrymae* is the way the music seems to enact the very loss it laments. The Middle Ages also had a central place for a story of darkness and death, the story of Christ's Passion. But that story, whether expressed in the Easter liturgy, in the miracle plays or in stained glass windows across Europe, does not stop with Christ's death on the cross. That death, terrible though it is, is but a moment in a larger story, one that will end with the Resurrection and the Last Judgement, a story the Middle Ages would have called, as Dante called his poem, a comedy, because it starts badly but ends well. When, in the sixteenth century, religion takes its inward turn, the shape of that story is lost. The world becomes a colder place.

Some will dismiss all this with the boo-word 'Hegelianism' and accuse me, along with Heller, Mann and the rest, of nostalgia or, worse, of proto-fascism, in our longing for an ordered world of community to contrast with the fragmented, liberal and individualistic world in which we live. Even Frank Kermode, a scholar noted for his openness to the new, once accused Eliot of being a closet Romantic for his notion of a moment when unity fragmented and 'sensibility' grew 'dissociated'. That there is a real issue here, and one that has to be faced head-on, is attested to by Eliot's career. His prose writings of the 1930s and 1940s do seem to spring from a longing for a once-unified Europe, and it is there that some of his most notorious anti-Semitic remarks occur. Does that then invalidate his insight into seventeenth-century poetry and culture? Does not everyone who responds to poetry know what he means when he contrasts Marvell's 'unified sensibility' with that of the poets who followed him? Is it not possible to separate the cultural critique from the nostalgia and the prescriptiveness of how a once-lost unity can be found again? T.J. Clark, the art historian, puts the problem most clearly when, in an early footnote to his splendid *Farewell to an Idea: Episodes from a History of Modernism*, he writes:

I realize that I shall be taken here and elsewhere to be idealizing pre-modern society, and inventing a previous watertight world of myth and ritual, agreed-on hierarchies, implicit understandings, embodied places, and so on. There is no easy way out of this dilemma. Of course pre-Modern societies (and certainly the ones existing in Europe immediately before the spread of mercantile capitalism and the seventeenth-century crisis) were conflicted and ideologically incomplete. I am on the side of historians who have fought against the picture of a pre-modern Europe characterised by absolute cultural uniformity, immovable religious consensus, the unthinkability of alternative views of the world, etc. Nonetheless, if we do not make a distinction between societies built, however inefficiently, upon instanced and incorporated belief, with distinctions and places said to be inherited from time immemorial, and societies driven by a new kind of economic imperative, in which place and belief are subject to constant revision by the very forces that give society form, then I reckon we forfeit the chance of thinking critically about the past two hundred years. To call such comparative thinking 'nostalgia' (or in the present techno-ecstatic conjuncture, 'Luddism') is just the latest form of philistinism about history in general.

Thomas Mann himself was well aware of the problem. In fact *Doctor Faustus* is nothing other than his desperate and impassioned struggle with it (as, in its way, is *The Magic Mountain*, written twenty years earlier). The source of Leverkühn's power as a composer, as well as his despair, is his recognition of the truth of Hegel's vision of a present in which the oracles are dumb, the social structures which made their existence possible having long since given way to modern capitalist individualism. On the other hand the Germany he inhabits, which is in the grip of a party which believes that it is possible to forge a new cultic and communal society in the post-industrial world, appals and terrifies him, as much as it does Zeitblom. Can one retain the critical insights, feel the loss as real, without at the same time opting for the demented Nazi vision of a new cult? This is the question out of which the tortured novelist, writing in distant California as the Nazi dream drags Europe to its destruction, forges one of his greatest works.

3

What Shall We Have To Drink In These Deserts?

Let me try to give a little more life to that striking phrase, 'the disenchantment of the world', by focusing on the work of a few artists, working from the early sixteenth to the early nineteenth centuries. I could have chosen others, but these will do both as examples and as a way of introducing some of the themes that will come into prominence when we turn to the modernism of our own time.

I want to begin with three sixteenth-century artists, and, first, with a visual artist and with a work made in 1514, three years, that is, before Luther nailed his ninety-five theses to the door of the Castle Church in Wittenberg. I do this because I want to show, among other things, that these intuitions of a change in man's relation to the world are not dependent on external events such as the Protestant and French revolutions, though of course these are important contributory factors, but that all are part and parcel of the same thing, the coming to the surface of tensions which had been growing for some time and which finally burst out into the open. In that year, 1514, Albrecht Dürer, recognised even in his lifetime as the greatest Renaissance artist of the North, made an engraving to which he gave the enigmatic title *Melencolia I* [*figure 1*]. An enormous brooding woman in flowing robes, with wings and a crown of leaves, sits leaning her head on her hand in an indeterminate space next to a ruined house against which a ladder is propped. An eerie moonlight blankets the scene and on the left, above a sheet of water, an ugly-looking bat spreads its wings, on which the mysterious title of the engraving is displayed. In her right hand the woman holds a compass and all around her lie other measuring instruments and tools: a pair of scales, a turned

figure 1 Albrecht Dürer, *Melencolia* I. Engraving, 1514.

figure 2 Albrecht Dürer, *St Jerome in his Study*. Engraving, 1514.

sphere of wood, a truncated rhombo-hedron, pliers, nails, a saw. On the wall behind her is an hourglass and next to it a magic square with a bell above it. From her belt, in equal disarray, hang a bunch of keys and an open purse. Sitting a little above her is a *putto*, busily scribbling. The two figures convey the overwhelming impression of tension and anxiety in the midst of what we para-doxically experience as both stasis and chaos.

In his great book on the artist Erwin Panofsky points out that the engraving must not be looked at in isolation. Dürer engraved two important works in 1514, *Melencolia I* and *St Jerome in his Study* [*figure 2*], and in every instance except one he gave them away as a pair. Indeed, Panofsky shows, they represent two contrasting views of life. The saint sits in his study, flanked by his animals. The room is bathed in warm sunshine. On the desk are only a crucifix and an inkbottle, while the saint's hat hangs on the wall behind him. Dürer has done everything within his power to render the room glowing, comfortable and warm. Even the hour-glass next to the hat and the skull on the table are less a threat than a reminder of man's natural end. The engraving represents a man redeemed from time not through the denial of time but through its acceptance; the saint who gave the Latin West its Bible is here shown at one with himself and with his God as he works, absorbed in his great task of transmission.

Even to the untrained eye the contrast with the *Melencolia* could not be greater. Panofsky's brilliant analysis of the iconog-raphy merely confirms one's instinctive feeling when faced with the two works. In every respect, he suggests, Dürer seems here to have wished to invert the *St Jerome*. The female figure with her useless wings represents art in competition with God. The Melencolia is a terrestrial craftsman cut off from all tradition and therefore incapable of productive work. 'As for geometry,' Panofsky quotes Dürer as saying, 'it may prove the truth of some things but with respect to others we must resign ourselves to the opinion and judgement of men.' This might appear a rather bland and neutral statement, but one can see what Dürer thinks of 'the opinions and judgements of men' when he says: 'The lie is in our understanding, and darkness is so firmly entrenched in our mind that even our groping will fail' – a full-blooded expression of the sense of solitude and desolation which,

Luther is to suggest, only an awareness of the saving grace of Christ can overcome.

This coexists in Dürer with a Humanist belief that the mastery of art consists of a combination of theoretical insights with practical skill. The one without the other is no use, he says, in a tone very like Leonardo's. Yet the fact remains that in this engraving what we have is something very different from the optimism of Florentine art. Melancholy is obviously thinking furiously, but is incapable of action, while the *putto* is scribbling furiously but we sense that what he is doing is of no value since it is quite without authority. Both the *putto* and Melancholy herself seem to be locked in a world in which there is simultaneously endless time and no time at all. They remind me of the mad energy without direction of Swift's Grub Street Hack in *A Tale of a Tub*, and of Hofmannsthal's Lord Chandos, hoping that by returning to the Ancients he will find a way out of his crisis, but

> I was unable to reach them . . . They were only concerned with each other, and the deepest, most individual part of my thought was excluded from their dance. In their company I was overcome by a feeling of terrible solitude; I felt like someone who had been locked into a garden full of eyeless statues.

Hence it seems to me that Panofsky is wrong to try and assimilate the engraving to the neo-Platonic theory of Saturnine genius so popular amongst the Florentine thinkers and artists. To them divine frenzy is all; though it brings melancholy in its wake it can nevertheless achieve great things. Indeed, melancholy is the hallmark of genius. This view of art and the artist has of course passed into the mythology of the Western world – think of our sense of Beethoven as the archetypal artist, a notion derived not from his music but from a vague memory of the rousing sound of his symphonies and from the endless reproductions of the busts and portraits of the deaf composer clearly in the grip of forces more powerful than himself. For Dürer, on the other hand, Melancholy is inactive, and this not because she is lazy but because all work has grown meaningless to her. Her considerable energy is paralysed not by sleep but by thought. She is reduced to inactivity and despair by the awareness of the insurmountable barrier separating her from the realm of Truth: 'The lie is in our understanding, and darkness is so firmly entrenched that even our groping will fail.'

It is no surprise to discover that Dürer's engraving, complete with hour-glass and magic square, figures in Mann's *Doctor Faustus*. Here the desire, even the need, to create comes to be seen not as a gift but as a curse. For while the desire to create seems to be the most natural thing in the world, something we are all born with, what is it in a world without sure relation to either tradition or authority but a meaningless self-indulgence? When the social trappings of art fall away, when patronage disappears and the artist is forced to compete in the market-place for the sale of his goods, can there be any justification for art other than the desire for money and fame? 'Why must I think that almost all, no, all the methods and conventions of art today *are good for parody only?*' asks Leverkühn (Mann's italics). Feeling himself to be destined for music, for the rich and creative life of the composer, he quickly becomes aware of the fact that in today's world there is no place for natural, spontaneous creation; everything we do seems false, laboured, second-hand; it feels like padding, pretence, a lie perpetrated by those who like to think of themselves as artists, in collusion with a market which knows that enough people need to feel they are in touch with some higher truth to make the art business profitable. In such a world the honest artist must either stop composing or seek in some way to deflect the terrible truth and, by a deal with the Devil perhaps, find again the springs of spontaneous creativity.

All that and more, it seems to me, is already implied in Dürer's two 1514 engravings: *St Jerome* shows us what has got lost; *Melencolia I* what we are left with.

Melancholy and despair are not, however, the only responses to this new situation. Or perhaps one should say that not all those who recognised what was at issue came from German-speaking lands. Two who had the encyclopaedic ambitions of a Dante or a Chaucer, but who sensed intuitively that the combined effect of the disappearance of a sacramental universe and the coming of print had changed the rules for ever, found in the new circumstances an unexpected opportunity for comedy. They were a Frenchman, Rabelais, and a Spaniard, Cervantes.

In Chapter 33 of *Gargantua* (1534) Rabelais presents us with the tyrant Picrochole and his generals, who are planning the destruction of the benevolent giant Gargantua, and the conquest of his territories. Very quickly their thoughts move from these limited objectives to grandiose schemes for the conquest of the whole world:

> Shall we see (said *Picrochole*,) *Babylon* and Mount *Sinai*? There is no need (said they) at this time, have we not hurried up and down, travelled and toyled enough, in having transfreted and past over the *Hircanian* sea, marched alongst the two *Armenias* and the three *Arabias*? By my faith (said he) we have played the fooles, and are undone: Ha, poor soules! What's the matter, said they. What shall we have (said he) to drink in these deserts? For *Julian Augustus*, with his whole Army died there for thirst, as they say. We have already (said they) given order for that. In the *Siriack* sea you have nine thousand and fourteen great ships laden with the best wines in the world: they arrived at *Port-Joppa*, there they found two and twenty thousand Camels . . .

Picrochole is acting as tyrants have always done, assuming that his wish and the facts will coincide and his courtiers hasten to reassure him, as courtiers have always done, that this is so. Rabelais draws our attention to this megalomania and makes comedy out of it by emphasising the mad logic of what is going on: Picrochole, already, in his mind, crossing the deserts of Arabia, suddenly becomes aware of the fact that his army will need water if it is to survive. In the world of the imagination, however, this is no problem: 'In the *Siriack* sea', his courtiers reassure him, 'you have nine thousand and fourteen great ships laden with the best wines in the world'. In reality, though, Picrochole and his army are routed by Gargantua only a few miles from his palace.

In reality? No. In reality there is no Picrochole and there is no Gargantua, nor is there any palace. In strict reality these are only the words Rabelais has written, now read by us and transformed in our imagination. But by making of Picrochole such a blatant flouter of reality Rabelais nudges us into accepting his reality – as a mad tyrant.

Picrochole may be a figure of the tyrant, but he is also a figure of the artist in his new circumstances, cut off from tradition and without either the Muses or the rules of Christian iconography to guide him as they guided Homer and the medieval artist, and so having to fall back on his imagination. The imagination is quite capable of conjuring up whole worlds, but unfortunately these worlds are made up only of words and images. The writer, alone now in his room, puts these words down on paper and, a little later the reader, alone in *his* room, with only the printed book in his hands, is given the tools to recreate this world in his imagination. For Rabelais this new freedom of the imagination is not, as it was for Dürer in the *Melencolia*, a cause of despair; but it is not a reason for rejoicing either, as it was for the Florentine neo-Platonists and has been for the majority of those who have written about art in the West since then. Rather, it is a cause of laughter.

In the larger economy of the book the same principle is at work: instead of trying to persuade us of his omniscience as an author – who would, after all, only be a version of Picrochole – Rabelais puts before us a fictional author who is shown to us in all his fleshly weakness, thereby stressing rather than denying that he, the real author, is a man not essentially different from his readers – not an angel or a prophet or the custodian of tradition like St Jerome. In this way he creates a space for fiction based not on denial or repression but on open acknowledgement of the way things are. Thus in the Prologue to *Gargantua* he tells us that 'in the composing of this lordly book, I never lost nor bestowed any more, nor any other time then what was appointed to serve me for taking my bodily reflection, that is, whil'st I was eating and drinking'; and in the last chapter of *Pantagruel* (1532) he decides abruptly to bring his chronicle to a close because 'my head aches a little, and I perceive that the Registers of my braine are somewhat jumbled and disordered with this septembral juice'. Of course nothing tells us that this is how the real Rabelais felt, but we sense that he felt more like that than like Picrochole or Dürer's St Jerome: felt, that is, more as we would feel were we to try and write a book without any guide other than our imaginations.

Cervantes too opens his encyclopaedic prose narrative, the first part of which was published in 1607 and the second in 1616, by insisting on the purely arbitrary and private nature of *his* creation:

> Idle reader, without my swearing to it, you can believe that I
> would like this book, the child of my understanding, to be the

most beautiful, the most brilliant and the most discreet, that anyone could imagine. But I have not been able to contravene the natural order; in it like begets like. And so what could my barren and poorly cultivated wits beget but the history of a child who is dry, withered, capricious, and filled with inconstant thoughts never imagined by anyone else.

Cervantes' reader is idle, *desocupado*, one who is not occupied, has nothing better to do. Unlike the listener to Homer or the reader of Dante, who listens or reads so as to have reaffirmed the order of things, *how things are*, this reader is imagined as turning the pages of a printed book in the solitude of his or her own room, simply in order to pass the time. And the author too, though he would like to be the inspired spokesman of the community, recognises that he is only a solitary individual, 'filled with inconstant thoughts never imagined by anyone else', and therefore with no authority for what he says and no access to the truth or to a Muse who would herself have access to it. In such a situation the worst possible thing would be to imagine or pretend that he did; his only hope is to accept that this is the way things are and to make the best of them. In that way, perhaps, he may become the spokesman for a new community of solitary individuals.

Cervantes explains to the reader that he wished to offer him a prologue that would be 'plain, bare, unadorned by . . . the endless catalogue of sonnets, epigrams, and laudatory poems that are usually placed at the beginning of books'. Yet even something as simple as this seemed to be beyond him, he confesses, as though once the dead wood of convention had been banished there was actually nothing at all to put in its place:

> I picked up my pen many times to write it, and many times I put it down again because I did not know what to write; and once, when I was baffled, with the paper in front of me, my pen behind my ear, my elbow propped on the writing table, and my cheek resting on my hand, pondering what I would say, a friend of mine, who is witty and wise, unexpectedly came in and seeing me so perplexed asked the reason, and I hid nothing from him and said I was thinking about the prologue I had to write for the history of Don Quixote, and the problem was that I did not

want to write it yet did not want to bring to light the deeds of
so noble a knight without one.

The contrast seems to be between a traditional florid, mendacious
prologue, full of rhetoric and bearing no relation to the subject in
hand, and one which is completely true to it. But what appears to
happen is that if you banish the traditional preface you are left
not with the truth but with nothing. Robbed of his traditional
rhetoric, the writer too finds himself *desocupado*, without an occu-
pation, uncomfortably aware of his body precisely because he is
thrown back on himself and his private resources. This, at least is
what the Prologue shows. But what it *does* is something quite
different. For all this talk of being unable to say anything in effect
constitutes a new kind of prologue, which is at one and the same
time an examination of the absurdity of all prologues, a cry for
help, a plea for understanding, and an unusual but effective way
of starting an unusual book.

What happens when the story proper gets under way? At first
all seems to be well, if by well we mean that at last the story
proceeds as we expect stories to proceed. 'Somewhere in La
Mancha', the book begins, like many a respectable and self-
respecting novel, and though the next phrase is a little odd, we
skim over it and find ourselves where we want to be, in the midst
of a life and a world that are not our own:

> Somewhere in La Mancha, in a place whose name I do not care to
> remember, a gentleman lived not long ago, one of those who has a
> lance and ancient shield on a shelf and keeps a skinny nag and a
> greyhound for racing. An occasional stew, beef more often than
> lamb, hash most nights, eggs and abstinence on Sundays, lentils on
> Fridays, sometimes squab as a treat on Sundays – these consumed
> three-fourths of his income. The rest went for a light woolen tunic
> and velvet breeches and hose of the same material for feast days,
> while weekdays were honored with dun-colored coarse cloth. He
> had a housekeeper past forty, a niece not yet twenty, and a man-of-
> all-work who did everything from saddling the horse to pruning
> the trees. Our gentleman was approximately fifty years old; his
> complexion was weathered, his flesh scrawny, his face gaunt, and he
> was a very early riser and a great lover of the hunt.

Suddenly, though, a new note is struck:

> Some claim that his family name was Quixada, or Quexada, for
> there is a certain amount of disagreement among the authors who
> write of this matter, although reliable conjecture seems to indi-
> cate that his name was Quexana, but this does not matter very
> much to our story; in its telling there is absolutely no deviation
> from the truth.

Instead of happily entering into another world we are suddenly
made to face up to the fact that this world comes to us filtered
through 'the authors who write of this matter', and this intrusion
of scholarly precision, far from reassuring us, only serves to
fuel our anxieties. We did not open the book to be faced with this
but to be swept away by a story where questions of accuracy
would be suspended. For the duration of the story, at least, we
wanted to be able to have total confidence in the narrator and not
to have to think about whether he was, like Homer, privy to the
Muses or not.

Yet we read on and are soon reassured: the phrase 'our story'
suggests a tale honed by tradition, one belonging not to a single
author but to a community, and even if we know that what we are
reading is not an aural narrative told by the village story-teller but
a tale invented for our delectation by one man, we find reassur-
ance in that first person plural. Yet the bland conclusion, that 'in
its telling there is absolutely no deviation from the truth', far from
reassuring us, only raises questions about the confidence we can
place in this narrator who at one and the same time tells us he
'does not care to remember' where exactly his hero came from,
that he isn't sure of his name, and that his story is true in every
respect. What, we wonder, can he possibly mean by truth?

However, the story picks up again, to present us with the
central fact about 'our hero' – that he spent all his time reading
books of chivalry, neglected the administration of his estate and in
the end loses his mind, becomes 'so convinced in his imagination
of the truth of all the countless grandiloquent and false inventions
he read that for him no history in the world was truer', and then
takes the final step and determines 'both for the sake of his honor
and as a service to the nation, to become a knight errant and travel

the world with his armour and his horse to seek adventures and engage in everything he had read that knights errant engaged in'. To that end he digs out an old suit of armour and polishes it up, finds a suitable name, Rocinante, for his old nag, and then, 'having given a name, and one so much to his liking, to his horse, he wanted to give one to himself, and he spent another eight days pondering this, and at last he called himself Don Quixote'. To this he adds the suffix of 'la Mancha', 'thereby, to his mind, clearly stating his lineage and country and honouring it by making it part of his title'.

There is something deeply unsettling about this. We do not want heroes of novels to give themselves their names; we want the author to do that. For by giving himself a name the hero of this novel opens up an uncomfortable gap between himself and his name. We grasp the name but we want to grasp the self. We know that names are arbitrary things, given by parents; but that is the point: they are given, not assumed. Only confidence men give themselves their names, but Don Quixote is anything but a con man. Who then is he? As Marthe Robert points out, by choosing a name for himself, Don Quixote brings out into the open all the contradictions that have been building up about what it is we are reading and sets the tone for the rest of the book. Don Quixote, she argues, deflects the destiny of the novel he is in, which should have been about an impoverished country gentleman in the backwoods of Castile (we can easily imagine a nineteenth-century Spanish novel of this kind) and turns it before our eyes into something much stranger and more arresting, an exploration of the nature of novels and their ontological status.

This has not been well understood. The standard view of the novel, most recently expounded by Adam Thirlwell in *Miss Herbert*, a book I will return to in a later chapter, is that it is a critique of idealism. The example is often taken of one of the first episodes, that of Don Quixote's freeing a boy who is being beaten by his master. He orders the man to pay the boy his wages and let him go. The man accepts but says that as he has no money on him the boy must come with him 'and I'll pay him all the *reales* he deserves'. The boy protests. If I go with him, he says, he's going to beat me even harder. Don't worry, Don Quixote grandly reassures him, as long as he gives me his word you have nothing to fear. Many chapters later Don Quixote and Sancho Panza meet the boy again, and the don explains that here is a living example of 'how important it is that there be knights errant in the world to right the wrongs and offences committed by the insolent and evil men who live in it'. The boy, however, has another view. He explains that as soon as Don Quixote had left them the man tied him up again and beat him harder than ever:

> Your grace is to blame for everything, because if you had continued on your way and not come when nobody was calling you or mixed into other people's business, my master would have been satisfied with giving me one or two dozen lashes, and then he would have let me go and paid me what he owed me.

This, Thirlwell claims, is the essence of the novel, 'the juxtaposition of chivalrously good intentions with the prose of real life'.

That is certainly one strand in it. But to see it as the main strand is to assimilate this strange and powerful novel too easily to a certain tradition, one which sees the novel as replacing the idealism of poetry with a new realism. Cervantes, like Rabelais, finds the form more troubling, as the Prologue has suggested. His stroke of genius was not the relatively obvious one of parodying, through his hero, the romances of the time, or even idealism in general, but of doing precisely what he said he had done in the Prologue, creating a hero who is in some essential way like himself. Those who see the don as an exemplar of an outdated idealism, and therefore feel comfortably superior to him, choose to disregard what Cervantes ruefully says in the Prologue: 'I have not been able to contravene the natural order; in it, like begets like. And so what could my barren and poorly cultivated wits beget but the history of a child who is dry, withered, capricious, and filled with inconstant thoughts never imagined by anyone else?' The critique of idealism we find in the novel is so troubling precisely because the primal idealisation is the conception and execution of the very work in which the critique is made.

Don Quixote and Picrochole are distant cousins, and both are also, as it happens, closely related to Cervantes and Rabelais. Don Quixote's madness makes of him a kind of fundamentalist, someone who is determined to find meaning in a world where it is difficult for the rest of us to see it. As with the fundamentalist, the person who is convinced that Bacon wrote Shakespeare's plays, or the anti-Semite, nothing crosses his consciousness that cannot be seen in the terms in which he has chosen to view the world. If a giant turns out to be a windmill, or his beloved Dulcinea a peasant girl, that is only because enchanters have been fiddling with the way the world appears; in reality he knows they are of course a giant and Dulcinea. But, as Cervantes is fully aware, there is a sense in which windmills, peasant girls, giants and Dulcinea are all equally unreal, all the products of one man's imagination, and to take fictional windmills and peasant girls as being real is as much of a leap of faith as to take them as being giants and Dulcinea.

Don Quixote's madness dramatises for us the hidden madness in every realist novel, the fact that the hero of every such novel is given a name merely in order to persuade us of his reality, and that he has giants created for him to do battle with and Dulcineas for him to fall in love with simply to satisfy the demands of the narrative. And it dramatises the way we as readers collude in this game because we want, for the duration of our reading, to be part of a realised world, a world full of meaning and adventure, an *enchanted world*. It is no coincidence that the novel emerges at the very moment when the world is growing disenchanted. We need enchantment and are prepared to pay good money to get at least a dose of it. The profound irony of *Don Quixote* is this: that as we read about the hero's obvious delusions we believe that we are more *realistic* about the world than he is, less enchanted, whereas we are of course ourselves in that very moment caught in Cervantes' web and enchanted by his tale.

Or not quite. Cervantes enchants us and then, as we have seen, periodically pulls the rug (the magic carpet?) from under our feet. And he does this partly in order to remain honest and partly in order to remind us that the world is no longer enchanted. This is no easy task, because there are powerful elements within us which want to deny this. But it is a task he relishes.

Towards the end of Chapter VIII of Part I, which in Cervantes' original division of his book concluded Part I, a Basque squire picks a quarrel with Don Quixote and this quickly escalates into a full-blown fight:

Don Quixote was charging the wary Basque with his sword on high, determined to cut him in half, and the Basque, well-protected by his pillow, was waiting for him, his sword also raised, and all the onlookers were filled with fear and suspense regarding the outcome of the great blows they threatened to give each other . . . But the difficulty in all this is that at this very point and juncture, the author of the history leaves the battle pending, apologising because he found nothing else written about the feats of Don Quixote.

Some readers may be old enough to remember the sense of impotent outrage we used to feel when, at the climax of a film, something happened to the projector or the reel and the screen went blank, followed by the lights going on and apologies from the management together with the promise that everything would be in order soon and the film would go on. Something of that feeling now engulfs the reader of *Don Quixote*. This is the first we have heard about a manuscript on which the story depends, and though it has been prepared for as early as the Prologue, the sudden discovery that not only is this the case but that the manuscript has now petered out is devastating. The next chapter takes stock of the situation:

In part one of this history, we left the brave Basque and the famous Don Quixote with their swords raised and unsheathed, about to deliver two down strokes so furious that if they had entirely hit the mark, the combatants would have been cut and split in half from top to bottom and opened like pomegranates; and at that extremely uncertain point, the delectable history stopped and was interrupted, without the author giving us any information as to where the missing parts could be found.

The new author or editor, or whatever we choose to call him, now takes centre stage, telling us that this caused him no end of grief, though he was convinced that 'it seemed impossible and completely contrary to all good precedent that so good a knight should have lacked a wise man who would assume the responsibility of recording his never-before-seen-deeds'. He concludes sadly that only Time is to blame, 'Time, the devourer and consumer of all things, who had either hidden it away or consumed it'. However, as is the way with these things, one day when he is in the market in Toledo, a boy comes up to sell some notebooks and old papers to a silk merchant he is talking to, and he takes a look at one of them. Unfortunately it is in Arabic, so he needs a translator, but in Toledo these are not hard to find. It turns out that the book is entitled *History of Don Quixote of La Mancha Written by Cide Hamete Benengeli* (or, in good Castilian English, Mr Hamid Eggplant). Promptly buying the book, the 'editor' engages a Moriscan translator, who in barely a month and a half translates the entire history 'just as it is recounted here'.

However, though the editor tells us that 'no history is bad if it is true', he also has to admit that the author was an Arab, and 'the people of that nation are very prone to telling falsehoods'. Moreover, because they are such enemies of Spain, 'it can be assumed that he has given us too little rather than too much'. However, in the spirit of genial obtuseness which seems to characterise him, he concludes:

> In this account I know there will be found everything that could rightly be desired in the most pleasant history, and if something of value is missing from it, in my opinion the fault lies with the dog who was its author rather than with any defect in its subject. In short, its second part, according to the translation, began in this manner . . .

Thus we are to rely on a historian who belongs to a race of liars who is writing about one of his enemies, and on a translator who has put hundreds of pages of Arabic into Spanish in under two months. Yet such is the power of narrative that we soon forget all this, except, of course, when it suits Cervantes to remind us.

As Marthe Robert points out, and as I have been arguing, the book is not really a satire on popular romances, such as *Amadis of Gaul*, which at moments it purports to be. It is about our relation to tradition and about the place of art, and especially that most mysterious of arts, the art of narrative, in a world where disenchantment has eroded our confidence in the sacramental. Behind *Amadis*, as Robert rightly insists, looms the figure of Homer (just as behind the popular tales of the giants Rabelais parodies looms the book of Genesis). The author of *Don Quixote*, she says, is not, like the Homeric bard, a central component of an organisation where each one is, by virtue of tradition, both the *protégé* and the protector of order, but a solitary individual, answerable to no-one but himself, without any faith other than his experience, without any guide other than his intuition.

This reminds one of Walter Benjamin's remarks on the difference between the novel and its predecessor, the oral tale:

What differentiates the novel from all other forms of prose literature – the fairy tale, the legend, even the novella – is that it neither comes from oral tradition nor goes into it. This distinguishes it from storytelling in particular. The storyteller takes what he tells from experience – his own or that reported by others. And he in turn makes it the experience of those who are listening to his tale. The novelist has isolated himself. The birthplace of the novel is the solitary individual, who is no longer able to express himself by giving examples of his most important concerns, is himself uncounseled, and cannot counsel others. To write a novel means to carry the incommensurable to extremes in the representation of human life.

And he at least understands *Don Quixote*'s role in the transition from the world of the story-teller to the world of the novelist: 'Even the first great book of the genre, *Don Quixote*, teaches how the spiritual greatness, the boldness, the helpfulness of one of the noblest of men, Don Quixote, are completely devoid of counsel and do not contain the slightest scintilla of wisdom.'

And just as the book tells us of the onset of the hero's madness and attributes it to his reading too many books on chivalry, so it describes its passing. At the end, as he lies dying, Don Quixote finally admits to himself, and to those around him, that he has been mistaken all along, and he dies recognising the folly of his quest, the madness of his desire to find meaning in everything in the world. But by this time, of course, as with the Prologue, his life has been lived and the book of his adventures completed.

Just as the discovery of the figure of Panurge, a little way into *Pantagruel*, the first of the five books to be written by Rabelais, seems to have freed Rabelais to pursue his epic and encyclopaedic ambitions with a free heart, so the invention of the Knight of the Mournful Countenance seems to have allowed Cervantes to move from the lazy and sluggish author unable and unwilling even to write a Prologue, to the writer we know and love. His insight lay in his grasp of how Don Quixote's invention of himself, his forcing himself into a role to be played for the duration of his life, both is and need not be (quite) a mirror of the writer's. At the end the poor knight cannot keep it up, and at his death has to admit that he behaved like a fool, that there were no real grounds for any of his actions. The writer admits as much from the start as we have seen. The extraordinary quality of the book, what gives it its status as both the first novel and the first anti-novel, depends on the fact that by doing so he allows the book to keep moving and the nature of the hero's character and adventures to see the light of day. The real protagonists, though, are the writer and the reader, who both undergo adventures enough to last them a lifetime, even if neither ever quite understands what these are.

4

Anxiety Is The Dizziness Of Freedom

One cannot look at Dürer's *Melencolia I* or read a chapter of
Rabelais or Cervantes without sensing that they knew in their bones
that they were living through a period of decisive change. Every
major artist of the time sensed this, but most, from Leonardo to
Michelangelo, from Petrarch to Spenser, saw only the opening up of
new possibilities as older traditions crumbled and were swept away.
The repressive tyranny of the Church was being destroyed and
Protestantism had got rid of old superstitions while Humanism gave
the individual a new freedom to express himself – that at least is the
myth that was perpetuated by both Protestantism and Humanism,
and one that in its simplicity and apparent self-evidence still shapes
the popular imagination. Throughout the last century, though, and
often under the impetus of Modernism itself, this picture has slowly
been eroded. It now seems clear that what happened was that
Protestantism and Humanism between them brought into being the
world picture that was to dominate the following three centuries, a
picture that seemed to explain everything and that propelled Europe
into leading the world in science and technology, but that really was
only *a* picture of the world. Artists who felt ill at ease in the dominant traditions started to look behind that picture to the Middle
Ages or beyond it to Africa, Japan or Bali, while historians, anthropologists and cultural analysts began to discover that cultures other
than the dominant one were anything but benighted and barbaric,
were in fact highly sophisticated and rich in tradition, though the
premises on which their world pictures were based were radically
different from those of the West.

As historians have increasingly been showing, and as I suggested
in my discussion of the two Dürer engravings, the disenchantment

of the world was not something that happened overnight, or even in the decade between 1517 and 1527. Things were quite different with the French Revolution. No-one in Europe had any doubt that something decisive, whether wonderful or terrible, had happened in 1789. What the Revolution did was give everyone the sense that even the most ordinary life could be changed. You were not stuck for ever in the place or the role into which you had been born. Everyone was now equal and everyone, in principle, had equal opportunities. By the time Napoleon was crowned Emperor not only did every soldier feel that he had a field-marshal's baton in his knapsack, every citizen felt that he too could be Emperor. 'Among the eminent persons of the nineteenth century,' wrote Emerson many years later, 'Bonaparte . . . owes his predominance to the fidelity with which he expresses the tone of thought and belief, the aims of the masses of active and cultivated men.' He owed his success, Emerson continues, entirely to the fact that he asked help of no-one, that he did things his own way. 'I should have done no good if I had been under the necessity of conforming to the notions of another person,' he quotes Napoleon as saying in 1796. In a world run by kings and rulers who had inherited their power and wealth, and who had no idea how to use it or what to do, 'here was a man who in each moment and emergency knew what to do next'.

> In the plenitude of his resources, every obstacle seemed to vanish. 'There shall be no Alps,' he said; and he built his perfect roads, climbing by graded galleries their steepest precipices, until Italy was as open to Paris as any town in France . . . Having decided what was to be done, he did that with might and main. He put out all his strength. He risked everything and spared nothing, neither ammunition, nor money, nor troops, nor generals, nor himself.

Unfortunately such a combination of qualities is rare; besides, there is only room for one emperor at any one time. What happened in post-Napoleonic Europe was that educated and ambitious young men found themselves in menial employment as badly paid tutors to the children of aristocrats, or as minor civil servants, when in their heart of hearts they felt it was their destiny to be

Napoleons. That is the fate of Stendhal's Julien Sorel. Above all it is the fate of Dostoevsky's characters. In Raskolnikov, the hero of *Crime and Punishment*, it is quite explicit: he is nobody, he cannot even earn enough to help his family, yet he senses that he is destined for great things, that he is a second, Russian, Napoleon. (The hero of *The Adolescent* wants to 'become Rothschild' – the principle is the same, for in the imagination of nineteenth-century Europe Rothschild was to finance as Napoleon was to war.) In the end, as the examining magistrate, Porphyry, explains to him, he murdered the old money-lender and almost asked to be caught for the simple reason that, like the rest of us, he prefers to be *someone*, even a murderer, than no-one at all. For the reverse side of the French Revolution was that, coinciding as it did with the growth of urbanisation and the drift to the cities, people who had once had a clear if lowly place in life, as farmers, masons, farriers or parish priests, now had none. That is the trouble with Dostoevsky's Underground Man. He wants to be pushed into the gutter because that will at least give him a sense that he exists, whereas living anonymously in the indifferent spaces of the modern city, he is not even sure that he does. That is the trouble with Emma Bovary and Anna Karenina, those tragic heroines of the post-Napoleonic age who are prepared to destroy their lives and those of the human beings close to them in order to feel they are alive. That is the trouble with Melville's Bartleby. He becomes a copyist in Wall Street but something in him rejects everything that that district, in the 1850s, is starting to stand for. Soon he stops even pretending to copy for his employer, and, when asked why, merely says: 'I would prefer not to.' In the end, of course, he is driven out of Wall Street and eventually dies, alone and unmourned, in the great cold metropolis of New York, that monument to the twin gods of the nineteenth century, Capital and Progress.

It is possible to recount a story of art and how it has developed since the 1790s which parallels this story of politics and people. Looking at music one could ask why it is that a composer like Haydn could write a hundred symphonies and only a few years later a composer no less gifted, no less industrious, Beethoven, could write only nine. The answer, quite simply, is that Haydn didn't feel he needed to start from scratch each time. Haydn is the last major composer to work as Dürer showed St Jerome working:

at ease within a tradition. What he had to do, to put it schemati-
cally, was to fill in a form. That he filled it in supremely well, far
better than any of his contemporaries except Mozart, is neither
here nor there. In a wonderful passage in Mann's *Doctor Faustus*,
Adrian Leverkühn tries to explain to his friend and future biographer how what happened to sonata form at this time encapsulates
what happened to music at large. When the form first developed,
he explains, there were clear rules governing its deployment: first
came an introduction, followed by a first theme, a second theme,
a development section, a recapitulation, and finally a coda. What
happens with Beethoven, argues Leverkühn, is that the development section, which had been 'a small part of the sonata, a modest
republic of subjective illumination', grows out of all proportion to
the rest till it overwhelms the whole, its growth synonymous with
the expression of the composer's demonic subjectivity. Even today
Beethoven's symphonies stand in the public imagination for the
most powerful expression of an individuality we all believe we
possess but which it is given to few of us to be able to express.

Unfortunately, after Beethoven (who, it will be observed, plays
in this story the role that Napoleon played in the previous one –
'In the plenitude of his resource, every obstacle seemed to vanish',
etc.) composers were left with nothing to hold on to except for
their individuality, and, without Beethoven's dynamism or optimism, this gradually led, in the course of the nineteenth century,
to an art more and more prone to stasis, dreaminess and disinte-
gration. Technically what happened was that the key system, on
which the classical sonata form had depended for its articulation,
was first tweaked in the interest of colour and originality, and then
gradually lost its power to control and started to seem unnatural
and artificial, yet without any other system being found to replace
it. The composer at the start of the twentieth century, an Arnold
Schoenberg or an Adrian Leverkühn, was thus caught between
repeating forms he could no longer believe in or trusting a subjectivity that was growing daily more problematic. And the same
trajectory could be described for the other arts, with Eliot and
Joyce, Cézanne and Picasso, taking the place of Schoenberg and
Leverkühn.

I will come to them in good time. For the moment I want to stay
with the paradoxes that emerged in the wake of the French

Revolution and Napoleon. The person who can best help us understand them, to my mind, is a reclusive genius who lived on the edge of Europe in the middle of the century, the Dane Søren Kierkegaard. In a dazzling torrent of works that seemed to burst out of him like a natural force in the decade between 1840 and 1849 (he was born in 1813), he produced what is in effect a kind of *Divine Comedy* of the nineteenth century. Dante, working in an age when an ordered universe was taken for granted, could build his poem out of a hundred cantos precisely (three canticles of thirty-three cantos plus a prologue) and place his sinners and saints in carefully graded positions in both Heaven and Hell, while drawing on a rich tradition to bring home to the reader how each of us can be saved and what steps need to be taken to find our way up the mountain of Purgatory. By 1840 all that has long gone. All Kierkegaard can do is to try and explore in every way imaginable the troubled heart and soul of nineteenth-century man, one who has been given his freedom twice over, first by God and then by the French Revolution, but who does not know what to do with it except torment himself with the sense that he is wasting his life.

Already in his first mature work *Either/Or* (1842), he had begun to explore what it might mean for a youth with brains and imagination to grasp that he was free to do what he wanted and to grasp at the same time that that freedom condemned him to a life of melancholy and inaction, as though the plethora of possibilities made all actualities seem pale and insubstantial. Coleridge of course had already sketched out such a fate in his examination of and identification with Hamlet. Kierkegaard carries on the work in a much more rigorous but also much more ironic manner, since the Hamlet-like young man who ostensibly writes the essays that make up Part I, the 'Either' of the title (it is probable that they were Kierkegaard's own early essays, given new life by being set in a new context), is pitted against a mature married man, a Judge, who speaks in Part II ('Or'), arguing that all the young man has to do is make just one choice, that of a partner for life, and all his problems will be solved, his agony and frustration will drop away and happiness will be his for ever. In a sense this was the alternative Dürer presented in his two engravings, but one feels that St Jerome is at least an imaginative possibility for Dürer, whereas the Judge is a wooden figure in whom neither the reader nor the author can quite believe. And that for a simple reason. He has really no response to the young man's question: What determines my choice of partner, and, if it is simply a matter of choosing rather than of the person one chooses, how is one to decide whom to choose? To say that God will provide, or that when that person turns up it will be obvious, is not to answer the young man at all; on the other hand, to say that it doesn't matter whom one chooses, that once she is chosen and becomes a partner for life all will be well, still does not answer the question and, besides, is not quite the sort of thing the Judge seems to want to endorse. On the other hand, in an abstract way, it is clear to the young man that the Judge is right: if only he himself was on the other side, had already chosen, he too would be like the Judge and all would be well. But he is not, and he doesn't know how to get to the other side, given his ironic and sceptical attitude to all choice.

The problem presented in *Either/Or* is essentially the problem the young Adrian Leverkühn resolves, in Mann's novel, by making his pact with the Devil. Too cold or too clear-sighted to go on playing the game of composition as Strauss and Mahler are playing it, yet desperate to compose, he needs something that will carry him over to the other side, as it were, give him back the excitement of composition. Stravinsky found that something in the Orthodox Church; a novelist like Muriel Spark in the Catholic Church; for a German Protestant like Leverkühn perhaps it could only be the Devil. Kierkegaard, though, went on believing that it had to be God. If he could only work his way through the Romantic disease of excessive freedom, he knew God would be waiting for him. But how? Two years after *Either/Or* he devoted an entire work to this mysterious disease. He called it *The Concept of Anxiety*. Anxiety, he points out, is to be distinguished from fear. Fear refers to something definite, 'whereas anxiety is freedom's actuality, the possibility of possibility'. This opaque formulation is partly elucidated by the later examination of 'the anxious possibility of being able' and of the fact that 'anxiety is the dizziness of freedom'. But however suggestive some of his phrasing is, the book remains relentlessly abstract. Five years later though, in *The Sickness Unto Death*, he hits upon a method that will do justice to his subject.

He begins from the obvious fact, also highlighted by Dostoevsky in *Notes from Underground*, that Plato misunderstood the nature of

man since he held that sin is ignorance and can therefore be rect-
ified by knowledge, whereas Kierkegaard and Dostoevsky follow
St Augustine in believing that sin is a misdirection of the will. The
grim refrain of *Notes from Underground* is that man is a perverse
creature who will often do things he knows will harm him merely
to prove to himself that he is alive and free. The classic example is
the young Augustine's attempt to steal the pears from the orchard
when he knows it is wrong, because he is driven by some powerful
inexplicable impulse to do so. Hell, as Dante brings out so powerfully, is the fall into despair because we both want and do not want
to do certain things, just as the addict both wants his drug and,
clearly aware that it is ruining him, does not want it. Why some will
allow the wanting to triumph and others will be able to overcome
it is a mystery, one that the Augustinian tradition fully respects. For
Kierkegaard it is the problem of the young man and the Judge
translated into a religious dimension. To deal with it he adopts what
he calls 'the dialectic method', his version of that Hegelian method
he both admired and loathed. This means always seeing the topic
under consideration alongside its opposite, never allowing it to take
centre stage alone. Thus man, he says, is a synthesis of finite and
infinite, temporal and eternal, freedom and necessity. He begins his
discussion of possibility and necessity, for example, with the point
that 'a self that has no possibility is in despair, and likewise a self
that has no necessity'. This he proceeds to develop in almost
musical fashion:

> Now if possibility outstrips necessity, the self runs away from
> itself in possibility so that it has no necessity to return to. This
> then is possibility's despair. Here the self becomes an abstract
> possibility; it exhausts itself in floundering about in possibility,
> yet it never moves from where it is nor gets anywhere, for
> necessity is just that 'where' . . . Thus possibility seems greater
> and greater to the self; more and more becomes possible
> because nothing becomes actual. In the end it seems as though
> everything were possible, but that is the very moment that the
> self is swallowed up in the abyss.

Remember Picrochole? And Dürer's *Melencolia*? Do the
words not apply perfectly to them? 'In the end it seems as though

everything were possible, but that is the very moment that the self is swallowed up in the abyss.' What the self lacks here is necessity. And wherein does necessity lie? 'What is really missing', says Kierkegaard, 'is the strength to obey, to yield to the necessary in one's self, what might be called one's limits.' But here we come up against the same problem as that which rendered the Judge's side of the argument so unconvincing in *Either/Or*. It was much easier to find one's own limits when there were external limits in place, precisely those limits which began to be called into question in the Renaissance and the Reformation and which had been abolished once and for all, in principle at least, by the French Revolution. In the modern world necessity seems too often a form of imprisonment rather than release, 'for without possibility it is as though a person cannot draw breath'. Thus 'necessity's despair is to lack possibility'. Is this not a striking analysis of the situation Raskolnikov finds himself in? And Emma Bovary? But – and this is why we must stick to the dialectical method – at the same time possibility's despair is to lack necessity. That is why when Raskolnikov or Emma Bovary or Anna Karenina acts, not tragedy but a kind of dreadful farce ensues. Agamemnon may, in his wife's eyes, have been wrong to sacrifice their daughter; Clytemnestra, in her son's eyes, may have been wrong to murder her husband: but in each case they were driven by an objective and clearly defined necessity – to allow the fleet to sail and thus fulfil his obligation as brother of Menelaus and commander of the Greeks on his part, to avenge the murder of her daughter on hers – and thus what ensues is tragedy. The contrast with Raskolnikov, Emma and Anna could not be clearer.

In the later portions of his book Kierkegaard explores 'the despair of not wanting to be oneself' as well as 'the despair of wanting in despair to be oneself'. Not surprisingly, he finds confirmation of his insights not in other philosophers, who have rarely recognised the unfathomable complexities of the self, but in the poets, and especially in Shakespeare. Not *Hamlet*, this time, but *Macbeth*. 'It is a psychological master-stroke', he remarks, 'that Shakespeare has Macbeth say (Act III, Scene 2): "Things bad begun make strong themselves by ill." In other words, sin has an inner consistency and in this consistency of evil it also has a certain strength.' And again, quoting the lines in Act II, Scene I,

'For from this instant [the murder of Duncan] there's nothing serious in mortality: All is but toys: renown and grace is dead.' 'What is masterly is the double stroke in the final words (renown and grace)', he comments. Here Kierkegaard is drawing attention to the brilliance with which Shakespeare, in three words, conveys Macbeth's loss of both public and private realms, the older, Homeric realm of *kleos*, fame, honour among one's peers, and the newer, Christian realm, in which one is alone before God, on whose grace one's eternal life depends.

Though Kierkegaard sets out *The Sickness Unto Death* as an argument built up step by step, it is difficult, unless perhaps one is his kind of Christian, to follow it as such. Rather, it seems to me, the book is a compendium, an encyclopaedia of the sickness that has befallen man in the nineteenth century. On every page there are remarkable formulations, worth any number of books on Romanticism or Modernism, such as: 'If one wants to compare running astray in possibility with the child's use of vowels, then lacking possibility is like being dumb. The necessary is as though there were only consonants, but to utter them there has to be possibility.' Does this not provide us with a way of grasping the mixture of silence, confusion and despair evident in so many of the greatest nineteenth-century novels – *Michael Kohlhaas*, *Madame Bovary*, *The Devils*? In fact, as we will see, whatever aspect of Modernism we look at, Kierkegaard will be an invaluable guide.

5

I Heard The Murmur And The Murmuring Sound

But before we turn to Modernism proper it may be useful to take a slightly more extended look at an artist working in the heyday of the French Revolution. It is important to do this to give flesh to what might seem too abstract and general, just as we turned to Dürer, Rabelais and Cervantes to anchor the discussion of the sixteenth-century 'disenchantment of the world'. Wordsworth was born in the same year as Beethoven, 1770, and is perhaps, like him, so remarkable an innovator just because he was still rooted in the eighteenth century. He has much to teach us about the paradoxes of the freed imagination, that poisoned chalice passed on from Romanticism to Modernism. Precisely because he is not usually seen in this light he may help us get away from the clichés that everywhere impede a proper understanding of Modernism. At the same time I want to try and show that not just music and poetry but all the arts were profoundly affected by the changed climate of the last years of the eighteenth century, and so following the lead of one of his finest critics Joseph Leo Koerner, I propose to bring in the paintings of Caspar David Friedrich whenever it seems relevant to do so.

Part of the problem of getting to grips with Wordsworth and Friedrich is that both of them seem early on to jettison the notion of genre. A genre is a bit like a family: when you are with your family you do not have to explain who you are each time you enter a room; you are taken for granted. But families can seem constricting as well as enabling, and a moment comes when confidence in genre starts to wane. We have already seen this at work in the emergence of the strange new productions of Rabelais and Cervantes, and we have seen Cervantes playing with the whole business of the genre of the Prologue. But if we want a symbolic moment in the eighteenth-century perception of genre to mirror 14 July 1789, then we have it in Dr Johnson's criticism of Milton (in his Life of the poet, 1779) for choosing to express grief at the death of his friend Edward King in the form of a pastoral elegy. '*Lycidas*', says Johnson in his magisterial way,

> is not to be considered as the effusion of real passion; for passion runs not after remote allusions and obscure opinions. Passion plucks no berries from the myrtle and ivy, nor calls upon Arethuse and Mincius, nor tells of rough *satyrs* and *fawns with cloven heel*. Where there is leisure for fiction, there is little grief.

At this point it is clear that genre has come to seem, like aristocratic privilege, a false imposition rather than a natural condition. The subtitle 'epic' or 'comedy' or 'pastoral elegy' had prepared readers or spectators for what they were about to experience and helped the writer enter his subject and establish an agreement with the reader. Johnson, that great classicist who nevertheless was also open to changing conditions, would have none of it. Like Kierkegaard's young man, what tradition has to offer seems to him false and no longer to chime with how things are. And this is even more true of Wordsworth and Friedrich, who were, after all, born a full sixty years after Johnson.

Geoffrey Hartman has noted of one of Wordsworth's earliest poems, 'Lines Left upon a Seat in a Yew-Tree', that 'its value . . . does not seem to depend in any way on the recognition of the species to which it may belong', and later in the same essay he argues that 'Wordsworth's form appears to be self-generated rather than prompted by tradition; and the greater the poem the clearer the effect.' Koerner, for his part, poring over the two little paintings sometimes called 'Aus der Dresdner Heide I and II' (From the Dresden Heath I and II), comes to the conclusion that

> each picture depicts a radically unremarkable nature, purged of human meaning and therefore of any clear relation to yourself, within a composition so centralised and intensely focused that it appears endowed with a quite particular and momentous

significance. This significance eludes you, and you stand before the pictures as before answers for which the questions have been lost.

Koerner places this problem in the context of art history:

> Before Friedrich, pendant canvases like 'From the Dresden Heath I and II' would have been linked together as episodes in legend or history, as distinct stages within a natural cycle (Seasons or Times of the Day), as examples of discrete types of landscape (heroic, pastoral, elegiac, etc.), or as natural analogues to differing human characters or qualities (the Four Humours, the Five Senses). Each image would correspond to a separate category within a system whose perimeters coincide with the whole of nature humanity. . . Friedrich's two canvases, on the other hand, are paired as exemplary moments within a single continuity of experience: the artist's personal *Erlebnis* [experience] of landscape.

It's uncanny how easily Koerner's words about the German painter apply to the English poet. For from the start Wordsworth's best poetry defies genre because it is not *about* this or that but is rather the encapsulation in words of an event which has filled him with wonder and which remains – for him and for us – mysterious, incapable of being absorbed into any system. A good example is the little poem 'A Night-Piece', written in the richly productive year of 1798, though not published till 1815.

The poem begins with what seems like pure description:

> The sky is overcast
> With a continuous cloud of texture close,
> Heavy and wan, all whitened by the Moon,
> Which through that veil is indistinctly seen,
> A dull, contracted circle, yielding light
> So feebly spread that not a shadow falls . . .

But suddenly there is a double change: in the landscape being depicted and in our sense of where the focus of the poem lies. The two are connected:

At length a pleasant instantaneous gleam
Startles the pensive traveller while he treads
His lonesome path, with unobserving eye
Bent earthwards; he looks up – the clouds are split
Asunder, – and above his head he sees
The clear Moon, and the glory of the heavens.
There in a blue-black vault she sails along,
Followed by multitudes of stars, that, small
And sharp, and bright, along the dark abyss
Drive as she drives: how fast they wheel away,
Yet vanish not! – the wind is in the tree,
But they are silent; – still they roll along
Immeasurably distant; and the vault,
Built round by those white clouds, enormous clouds,
Still deepens its unfathomable depth.

The emergence of the moon from the clouds seems to conjure up the traveller, to us and even to himself, as though till that moment he had been walking without any awareness of himself and his surroundings, locked in his own thoughts, 'pensive', 'unobserving', in a sense 'not there'. But the sudden emergence of the moon makes him look up and the poem itself suddenly takes off from the flat, almost prose-like opening, into something powerful and grand, as the impact of the scene he now looks at in the sky calls forth (in recollection) a language which strives, successfully, to be commensurate with it. In one great sentence Wordsworth does what he does best, uses syntax to convey the unfolding of something majestic and beyond thought. Yet the majesty never turns into what the eighteenth century called 'the sublime', the vague and awesome; it achieves its own sublimity, rather, by remaining focused – the beautiful touch 'the wind is in *the tree*', not 'in *the trees*', and the powerful contrast between the sound of the wind and the silence of the stars, whose immeasurable distance from us is conveyed with effortless economy. The repetition of 'clouds' reminds us that the focus of the poem is the traveller, whose perceptions exist in time, not the sky, which is eternal. This is a poem about *experiencing* a vision, not, like Blake's prophecies, about a vision:

> still they roll along
> Immeasurably distant; and the vault,
> Built round by those white clouds, enormous clouds,
> Still deepens its unfathomable depth.

But the poem does not end there. It is important, indeed central, to it that we experience, with the traveller, both the onset of the vision and its end:

> At length the Vision closes; and the mind,
> Not undisturbed by the delight it feels,
> Which slowly settles into peaceful calm,
> Is left to muse upon the solemn scene.

There the poet wisely leaves it to us to decide what form such musings take. Though for Wordsworth the scene may be 'solemn', what it brings to the viewer is 'delight' settling slowly into 'peaceful calm'. And we realise that what we are reading is the reconstruction, later, of the experience, the experience being both the content of the poem before us and its trigger. For the traveller at the start would not have wanted or been able to write, closed in upon himself as he was. Only the parting of the clouds, the vision of the moon, making the bent traveller straighten and look up, leads us to the present, the poem we are now reading.

However, nature is not always the source of serenity and joy. The most powerful passages in the first books of *The Prelude* concern an altogether more frightening image of nature. Once, having stolen a woodcock from a snare set by someone else,

> I heard among the solitary hills
> Low breathings coming after me, and sounds
> Of undistinguishable motion, steps
> Almost as silent as the turf they trod. (I.321–4)

Another time, rowing out into the middle of a little-known lake from a boat he had untethered from its mooring place, he has the nightmarish feeling of something rising up from the horizon and coming after him faster than he can row:

> a huge peak, black and huge
> As if with voluntary power instinct,
> Upreared its head. I struck, and struck again,
> And growing still in stature the huge cliff
> Towered up between me and the stars, and . . .
> . . . like a living thing,
> Strode after me. (I. 378–85)

We could say that in both instances Wordsworth has simply given concrete shape to his feelings of guilt at having done something morally wrong. But that would be to misunderstand what is going on. What both instances do is to dramatise his sense of feeling a stranger in the landscape and of somehow inflicting harm on it precisely *because* he is a stranger, an intruder. No poem expresses this better than another of the little poems he wrote in 1798/9, 'Nutting'.

This time he sets out on a perfect day, 'One of those heavenly days that cannot die', a bag on his back, a nutting crook in his hand. Forcing his way through brambles and matted ferns he comes at last to

> one dear nook
> Unvisited, where not a broken bough
> Drooped with its withered leaves, ungracious sign
> Of devastation . . .

It was, he says, 'a virgin scene'. This he stands surveying for a while, 'Breathing with such suppression of the heart/ As joy delights in'. He sits down beneath the trees and feels like those who, 'after long/ And weary expectation, have been blest/ With sudden happiness beyond all hope'. What brings this joy is the sense of the spot never having been seen before by human eye and its being a place where the human voice has never been heard, a place 'Where fairy water-breaks do murmur on/ For ever'; and, as so often, it is the sound of water running deep in the earth that rouses his deepest feelings:

> And – with my cheek on one of those green stones
> That, fleeced with moss, under the shady trees,
> Lay round me, scattered like a flock of sheep –
> I heard the murmur and the murmuring sound.

But then – and typically Wordsworth does not try to explain the action, only record it with puzzled honesty – he rises up and in a fit of vandalism proceeds to destroy this earthly paradise, dragging down the boughs and tearing at the nuts upon them: 'and the green and mossy bower,/ Deformed and sullied, patiently gave up/ Their quiet being'. The child he was, he now recalls, turns from the 'mutilated bower', exulting in his new-found riches, and then feels 'a sense of pain when I beheld/ The silent trees, and saw the intruding sky'. The very quietness of the spot, which had been one of its sources of power, that which had allowed him to hear the revivifying murmur of the waters, is what he has destroyed, the silence turning now into a mute accusation, almost a sense of shame as the sheltered nook is opened up to the sky through his destructive act.

The poem is so shocking because we sense that it is not so much the act of violence which is seen as a rape of nature as the very presence of the child; the act merely dramatises what had been latent all along, just as Rabelais and Cervantes had merely brought out into the open the fact that a book is always written by a fallible human being. Indeed, with hindsight we could go further and say that for the two earlier writers as, later, for Kafka, the act of writing was itself seen as a kind of violation of the world, and had to be recognised as such. The paradox for Wordsworth is that only in the midst of nature does he feel fully himself, as in some sense he was created to be, and yet his very presence in nature robs it of precisely that which made it such a source of healing and joy. Is there a way of interacting with nature which is not destructive?

The answer, and it is 'yes', is to be found in another poem written in 1798 and later incorporated into *The Prelude*, 'The Boy of Winander'. It begins with the kind of blunt assertion that so often heralds Wordsworth's best poetry: 'There was a Boy'. At the same time it establishes the central theme of the poem, the interconnection between person and place:

> There was a Boy; ye knew him well, ye cliffs
> And islands of Winander! – many a time,
> At evening, when the earliest stars began
> To move along the edges of the hills,
> Rising or setting, would he stand alone,
> Beneath the trees, or by the glimmering lake;

And there, with fingers interwoven, both hands
Pressed closely palm to palm and to his mouth
Uplifted, he, as through an instrument,
Blew mimic hootings to the silent owls,
That they might answer him. – And they would shout
Across the watery vale, and shout again,
Responsive to his call . . .
      And, when there came a pause
Of silence such as baffled his best skill:
Then sometimes, in that silence, while he hung
Listening, a gentle shock of mild surprise
Has carried far into his heart the voice
Of mountain-torrents; or the visible scene
Would enter unawares into his mind
With all its solemn imagery, its rocks,
Its woods, and that uncertain heaven received
Into the bosom of the steady lake.

The boy interacts with the landscape and its inhabitants not by wilfully desecrating it but by becoming a part of it, calling forth the cry of the owls by using his own fingers and vocal chords, to which they joyously respond; and this leads in turn, in the silence that ensues, to a complete incorporation of the landscape into the boy and the boy into the landscape. Remember Mann's comments on echo in Monteverdi: 'The echo-effect, the giving back of the human voice as nature-sound, and the revelation of it *as* nature-sound, is essentially a lament: Nature's melancholy "alas", the lament of the nymphs as related to the echo.' But it is not lament here in Wordsworth, showing that art, in the hands of the greatest masters, will always find a way out of the impasses philosophy and cultural history reveal.

At his best Wordsworth makes syntax, rhythm and enjambment do most of the work, and here, ending one line on the word 'pause' and another on the word 'hung', he enfolds us too, as we read and feel the weight of the words and the rhythm, in the magical reciprocity: 'a gentle shock of mild surprise/ Has carried far into his heart the voice/ Of mountain-torrents'. The body – of the boy, of the poet, of the reader – becomes more than a thing, it itself becomes a landscape, a place of depths and secret springs and rivers as the forward drive of the syntax in the last part of this extraordinary sentence curves back on itself to mimic the description. There is much that could be said about the placing of 'uncertain' here: is the sky uncertain because it is reflected (though Wordsworth prefers the more human and affective term, 'received') in the lake? Because the sky does not have a surface like the lake? Or because the whole scene is already in some sense lodged in the mind and body of the boy – and of the reader?

The poem is not over, though. Wordsworth, as always, wishes to convey a visionary experience, but also, like Proust, to place that experience in the context of life. His poet is a man speaking to men, not the unacknowledged legislator of the world. The context in which this experience, this habitual experience ('many a time'), is placed, is as powerfully shocking as the experience itself: 'This boy was taken from his mates, and died/ In childhood, ere he was full twelve years old.' And the poet goes on to describe the place where he is buried, bringing back the word 'hangs', disturbingly, also in enjambment:

> Pre-eminent in beauty is the vale
> Where he was born and bred: the churchyard hangs
> Upon a slope above the village-school . . .

But the sentence, like that which ended the main part of the poem, changes direction and we are left with a final surprise:

> And, through that churchyard when my way has led
> On summer-evenings, I believe that there
> A long half-hour together I have stood
> Mute – looking at the grave in which he lies!

This part of the poem might look at first as though it were merely anecdotal and sentimental: this wonderful boy with his ideal relationship to the world in which he grew up died tragically young. But the poem, like the late piano sonatas and quartets of Beethoven or the paintings of Caspar David Friedrich, asserts a quiet authority, so that its eccentricities cease to be that and become as inevitable, as unquestionable and *there* as an outcrop of rock. The final image, of the poet silently contemplating the grave, in a curious way takes us back to the boy and the owls: the poet becomes the boy as the boy became the owls, by mimicking him in the very poem we have been reading. For, no less than Dante's *Commedia* and Proust's *A la Recherche*, this poem ends with the poet preparing to write what we have just been reading. To achieve that he too must be silent, must 'hang listening', in order to become a part of the landscape, a part of the cemetery, rather than intruding on it destructively, like the boy in 'Nutting'. Only then can he reproduce, in language, that murmuring of the underground waters which is for him the sound of life itself.

To arrive at that point he must also have understood that dying in childhood, far from being a mere accident, was the boy's destiny; or, to put it more neutrally, that death and life form part of the same warp and weft and must be grasped as one. That this is what the poem, at its deepest, is saying is confirmed by another group of poems written in those miraculous years, the so-called 'Lucy' poems, especially the greatest and most compressed of them:

> A slumber did my spirit seal;
>   I had no human fears:
> She seemed a thing that could not feel
>   The touch of earthly years.
>
> No motion has she now, no force;
>   She neither hears nor sees;
> Rolled round in earth's diurnal course,
>   With rocks, and stones, and trees.

Lucy, we learn from the other poems in the cycle, died, like the Boy of Winander, while still a child. What this poem asserts and the others merely hint at is that by dying she fulfilled herself and that now in death she really is what the poet always sensed her to be, as mortal and immortal as the earth itself. Wonderfully, he conveys that this is a dynamic, not a static state: she is not beneath the earth but, like the rocks and stones and trees, 'rolled round in earth's diurnal course', the passive verb here strangely active, or rather, managing – and this is the heart of Wordsworth's genius – to escape the grammatical distinctions of active and passive in order to convey a state where our grammar no longer applies. It is only when he is sealed off from the world in a slumber that itself resembles nothing so much as death that the poet can grasp what Lucy really is. No less than Rilke, Wordsworth suggests that we diminish life by denying death.

Hence Wordsworth's solitaries, and the problems Wordsworth experiences in talking about them. The overt lesson of 'Resolution and Independence' is that simple poor people bring light to our complicated lives because they are contented with their lot. But the poem implies something quite different. It says that the Leech-Gatherer, first seen as resembling a stone lying in the landscape, is, like Lucy, a figure who touches the poet's heart because he exists beyond language, beyond most of what we think of as making up a man, and has started to merge with nature.

This figure of the solitary in Wordsworth takes many forms. Often he is an 'old man travelling', walking the country roads, or a lonely farm dweller. But sometimes the human beings who arouse a powerful feeling in the poet are very strange indeed. In Book VII of *The Prelude*, for example, once, when he was lost in some outlying part of London,

> I was smitten
> Abruptly, with a view (a sight not rare)
> Of a blind Beggar, who, with upright face,
> Stood, propped against a wall, upon his chest
> Wearing a written paper, to explain
> His story, whence he came, and who he was.
> Caught by the spectacle my mind turned round
> As with the might of waters; an apt type
> This label seemed of the utmost we can know,
> Both of ourselves and of the universe;
> And on the shape of that unmoving man,
> His steadfast face and sightless eyes, I gazed,
> As if admonished from another world. (VII. 637–49)

We are in Beckett country here. But also in Hofmannsthal country. Remember Lord Chandos's:

For it is something that has never been named and that is prob-ably impossible to name, which manifests itself to me at such moments, taking some object from my everyday surroundings, and filling it like a vessel with an overflowing torrent of higher life . . . A watering-can, a harrow left abandoned in a field, a dog in the sun, a poor churchyard, a small farmhouse – any one of these can become a vessel for my revelation.

These objects move him, we now see, precisely because they have somehow returned to the earth, because they do not belong to the unnatural human urge to use the world merely as a natural resource, are as far as it is possible to be from 'civilisation'.

What causes the poet's mind to turn 'as with the might of waters' is not just the stillness of the man and his sightless eyes, but the combination of those eyes with the paper pinned to his chest. Why should this combination affect him in this way though? Wordsworth does not explain, or rather fobs us off with the trite observation that this is a kind of emblem of our condition, showing us 'the utmost we can know,/ Both of ourselves and of the universe'. But is that quite right? It seems rather as though the image forces us to recognise our folly in thinking that we can understand who we are and control our own destinies. Our eyes are sightless and our stories are pinned to our chests, readable to the world but never to ourselves. There is a grandeur to the man which is close to that of Oedipus when, in Sophocles' last play, he goes to his death at Colonus. He moves the poet as does the sudden appearance of the moon as the clouds part or the vision of a mountain reflected in a lake, because, like them, he leads the poet out of himself and his thoughts and anxieties to a renewed and totally unsentimental understanding of his place in the universe.

The last book of *The Prelude* begins with a different kind of vision. The poet has decided to climb Mount Snowdon at sunrise with a group of friends. A thick fog hangs over the mountain as they begin the ascent. He is in the lead,

When at my feet the ground appeared to brighten,
And with a step or two seemed brighter still;
Nor was time given to ask or learn the cause,
For instantly a light upon the turf
Fell like a flash, and lo! As I looked up,
The Moon hung naked in a firmament

> Of azure without cloud, and at my feet
> Rested a silent sea of hoary mist.

The tops of the mountains rise up like so many hills out of this sea of mist, but the sky is wonderfully clear; the Moon has banished the stars and seems to gaze

> Upon the billowy ocean, as it lay
> All meek and silent, save that through a rift –
> Not distant from the shore whereon we stood,
> A fixed, abysmal, gloomy breathing-place –
> Mounted the roar of waters, torrents, streams
> Innumerable, roaring with one voice!
> Heard over earth and sea, and, in that hour,
> For so it seemed, felt by the starry heavens. (XIV. 35–62)

The Prelude does not quite end here. As always, the poet wishes to place the vision within the continuum of human life. And this is important. Joseph Koerner has some remarkable pages, in his book on Friedrich, about the painter's fondness for what he calls the *Rückenfigur*, the figure who is and is not the painter, who is and is not the viewer, who stands at the limit of the picture, with his back to us, so that what we see is not what he sees, but *him seeing*. It is very important to Friedrich, Koerner points out, that this figure should be there, for he reminds us that vision is always vision at a particular moment, from a particular place, and that though vision may be the goal it does not subsume life but is only one moment, one experience, within life. And it is also very important that this figure should be, as he is for Wordsworth on Snowdon, bathed in mist, for mist is what unites the elements of the picture, what brings individual and vision into one orbit. It is also, of course, a figure for paint itself, which conceals the canvas and reveals figures, yet is the medium in which the entire scene exists. '*Wanderer above the Sea of Fog*' (*figure 3*), writes Koerner, 'stands suspended between two notional paintings: on the one hand, the total replication of a valley in all its detail that has been overpainted in white; on the other hand, a blank canvas in which have begun to appear, here and there, the fragments of a scene.' What this is saying, I take it, is that such Romantic artists

figure 3 Caspar David Friedrich, *Wanderer Above the Sea of Fog, c.* 1818.

as Friedrich (and Wordsworth) are not so much visionaries as explorers of what it means to see and what it means to paint or write. They approach the final vision, the apocalyptic covering of the earth by water, the merging of self and landscape, with mingled excitement and apprehension, but something tells them to stop, to wake up before the earth is engulfed, to remain on firm land gazing into the mist beyond. 'In the end,' Kierkegaard had written in *The Sickness Unto Death*, 'it seems as though anything were possible, but that is the very moment that the self is swallowed up in the abyss.' Friedrich and Wordsworth point us to that moment but step back from the final annihilation. Perhaps it is their eighteenth-century roots. Perhaps it is their temperament. The result is to leave them – and us – with a sense of loss at what has not quite been surrendered to, but also exaltation at the memory of what was experienced. It leaves a place, too, for art, which is the activity by which the vision can be recaptured and the sense of loss anchored. In a difficult passage Koerner makes the case for Friedrich, relating his view of him to the later history of art. What he says holds also for Wordsworth, and gives us a template for assessing the complicated dance of art and vision, hand and eye, which is one central aspect of the history of Modernism: 'In the framed nothingness of *From the Dresden Heath*, or into the passage into loss plotted by *Fog*', he writes,

> Romantic landscape seems to prefigure the blinding and blinded project of twentieth-century abstraction, which is why Friedrich can figure as the origin of such histories as, for example, Robert Rosenblum's controversial *Modern Painting and the Northern Romantic Tradition*. If we submit Friedrich's art to the semiotics of Romanticism, however, we discern a far more complex state of affairs. Abstraction will always be only a passing moment in our experience of the image, just as Friedrich himself is often compelled to raise a cathedral above the last horizon of his spiritual 'histories', as modernity's return of the repressed. Yet neither does this return fully eradicate the moment of blankness.

II

MODERNISM

6

It's A Quick Death, God Help Us All

If Wordsworth and Friedrich abandon genre they nevertheless produce works which immediately assert that they are art and not something else, Wordsworth because he writes in verse, Friedrich because he paints in oils and frames his pictures. The novel's denial of genre was more radical. For the novel is precisely the form that emerges when genres no longer seem viable. From the start it pretended or pretended to pretend to be something else: a translation from a lost Arabic manuscript, the true account of the wreck of a boat on a desert island, the memoirs of a whore, a rake or an orphan. At the same time novels asserted, like Descartes at the start of his *Discourse*, that their creators would bow to no authority, would rely on nothing but themselves as honest and reasonable men. Genres were the sign of submission to authority and tradition, but the novel, a narrative in prose, was the new form in which the individual could express himself precisely by throwing off the shackles that bound him to his fathers and to tradition. It is no coincidence that so many eighteenth- and early nineteenth-century novels are precisely about young men refusing to do what their fathers wish, refusing to take on the roles that their fathers have mapped out for them. Yet usually the hero ends up inheriting after all, though on his own terms. And this alerts us to a paradox faced by the novel. For if it throws off all external authority, where does it get its own authority from? The answer has to be: from the inspiration or experience of the novelist himself. But who confers this authority upon him? No-one but himself. From the beginning, then, the novel was caught in the same double-bind as Don Quixote in giving himself a name and an epithet, asserting its truth and the value of what it was doing (which genre-derived works had never needed to do since it was the tradition that provided them with these things), yet knowing at heart that these were assertions and nothing more. Or perhaps not knowing but believing in the ability of the self to produce, and in the meaning and value of what is produced – that is what gives the works of Balzac and Dickens their sense of magisterial authority, and has made them the envy of many later novelists. Isaiah Berlin once called Verdi the last naïve artist, and in a sense the same could be said of Dickens and Balzac: none of them ever had any doubts about the nature of his vocation or his own ability.

In his essay on Verdi's naïveté Berlin identifies this with Schiller's use of the term in his contrast between the 'naïve' and the 'sentimental', but that seems to me misleading. Schiller's 'naïve' artist is one who belongs to what I have described as the world before its disenchantment in the sixteenth century. There are of course candidates for the term working long after 1600 – Benjamin examines one such in his essay on Nikolai Leskov, and the stories of Johann Peter Hebel would also probably qualify. The naïveté of Dickens, Balzac and Verdi is of a quite different kind. They were, after all, amongst the canniest operators ever known in their pursuit of popularity and success. I think John Bayley puts his finger on it in a brilliant essay on *Oliver Twist*. 'No novelist has profited more richly than Dickens from not examining what went on in his own mind', Bayley remarks. And though he rightly loves this aspect of Dickens, he is aware of its limitations. Dickens' novels, he suggests, lack the objectivity of the greatest art; their appeal is precisely that they remain in the realm of childhood nightmares, powerful precisely because such nightmares never really leave us:

> Iago and Verkhovensky are monsters because they know what they are doing; their actions let us loathe them and recoil from them into freedom, but we cannot recoil from Dickens' villains: they are the more frightening and haunting because we cannot expel them for what they do; they have the unexpungeable nature of our own nightmares and our own consciousness.

This is very fine. It catches the childish aspect of Dickens (as indeed of Verdi and Balzac) implied in the term naïve, in all its strength and its weaknesses.

Not having doubts is a blessed state, but it is not the same thing as having genuine authority. There is something hollow about Balzac, Dickens and Verdi compared with Dante or Shakespeare, but even compared with their older contemporaries, Beethoven and Wordsworth. It doesn't rest on their frequent clumsiness, for that is to be found in Beethoven and Wordsworth. It rests more on the very thing that is the root of their strength as artists and their enormous success as entrepreneurs: their inability to question what it is they are doing. In that sense they are the first modern best-sellers and in their work one can see the beginnings of that split between popularity and artistic depth which is to become the hallmark of modern culture.

But even as Balzac and Dickens were writing their spirited works, others were anxiously assessing what was really at issue. Chief among them, as I have suggested, was Søren Kierkegaard. His book *On Authority and Revelation*, though it deals with what he sees as a vital religious issue, is nevertheless a key work for understanding the artistic problems of the age. The book examines a curious case which had come to Kierkegaard's attention and which he felt to be, despite its superficial absurdity, exemplary. In the preface to a published volume of sermons a certain priest, Magister Adler, made the following claim:

> One evening I had just developed the origin of evil [*sic*], when I saw, illuminated by a flash of lightning, that everything depends, not upon the thought but upon the Spirit. That night a hateful sound went through our chamber. The *Saviour* bade me stand up and go in and write down the words.

However, when the authorities, in alarm, asked him to explain himself, he began a series of complicated defences, both insisting on the accuracy of what he had recounted and somehow diluting it, so that by the end it was no longer clear if what he had had was just a profound thought or an actual visit and instruction from Jesus. Kierkegaard saw this as what he called a 'bitter epigram upon our age', and wrote his book to tease out its implications. Essentially the point he is making is that we have today confused a genius and an apostle, a 'very great man' or a 'very great writer', and one who speaks with authority. If St Paul were to say to someone: 'Go, and do this', we could analyse his words till we were blue in the face and they would in the end turn out to be no different from the injunction you or I might give to someone: 'Go, and do this.' The difference lies in who we are, not in what we say. The difference lies in the fact that St Paul has authority and you and I have none. Kierkegaard sees what Dürer and Cervantes saw, that without authority we are reduced to claiming authority for ourselves when we know deep down that we have none. But, Kierkegaard feels, our age has not only lost access to authority, *it no longer even recognises the crucial distinction between one who has authority and one who only has genius.*

It is his preface that is of immediate relevance to us in our attempt to understand the nature of this new form, the novel. 'For it is one thing that a life is over, and a different thing that a life is finished by reaching its conclusion', he begins. A man, he goes on, may perhaps one day decide to become an author. But, says Kierkegaard,

> he may have extraordinary talents and remarkable learning, but an author he is not, in spite of the fact that he produces books . . . No, in spite of the fact that the man writes, he is not essentially an author; he will be capable of writing the first . . . and also the second part, but he cannot write the third part – the last part he cannot write. If he goes ahead naively (led astray by the reflection that every book must have a last part) and so writes the last part, he will make it thoroughly clear by writing the last part that he makes a written renunciation to all claim to be an author. For though it is indeed by writing that one justifies the claim to be an author, it is also, strangely enough, by writing that one virtually renounces this claim. If he had been thoroughly aware of the inappropriateness of the third part – well, one may say, *si tacuisset, philosophus mansisset* [had he kept quiet he would have remained a philosopher].

It could not be put more clearly. In our modern age, an age without access to the transcendental and therefore an age without any sure guide, an age of geniuses but no apostles, only those who do not understand what has happened will imagine that they can give their lives (and their works) a shape and therefore a meaning, the shape and meaning conferred by an ending. The task of those who have grasped the implications of this will be to try and bring home to those who haven't what it is that has been lost. Kierkegaard brings this part of his argument to an end with a pregnant aphorism: 'To find the conclusion it is necessary first of all to observe that it is lacking, and then in turn to feel quite vividly the lack of it.'

This dialectical movement is typical of Kierkegaard, and of Modernism. In his last great pseudonymous work, the *Concluding Unscientific Postscript* (1847), he describes, partly tongue in cheek, how, as a young man in Copenhagen, he would often sit in the beautiful Frederiksberg Gardens and ask himself what he should do with his life. The world is full of great new inventions, he would think, the telegraph, the steamship, the railway; what is there left to do for mankind? And then the thought came to him: what *he* could do was to make men aware of what they could *not* do! He could become the spokesman for the negative in this world that worshipped so many positives! However, he goes on, negativity is a very delicate thing; all too often even those who talk of negativity, by talking, turn it into its opposite:

> Among so-called negative thinkers, there are some who after having had a glimpse of the negative have relapsed into positiveness, and now go out into the world like town criers, to advertise, prescribe and offer for sale their beatific negative wisdom – and of course, a result can quite well be announced through the town crier, just like herring from Holstein . . . But the genuine subjective existing thinker . . . is conscious of the negativity of the infinite in existence, and he constantly keeps the wound of the negative open, which in the bodily realm is sometimes the condition for a cure.

Finding the conclusion means giving everything that has gone before a meaning. Simply giving something an end does not mean giving it a meaning, any more than a man's life acquires a meaning by coming to its end. To confuse a conclusion with a mere end is like confusing an apostle and a genius. Why it is so difficult to grasp exactly what novels do, how they work on us, is because novels look innocent, look artless. All they are doing is showing us ourselves in a mirror – or are they? Sartre, engaged in the same pursuit a hundred years later, teased out, with his usual rhetorical brilliance, the implications of Kierkegaard's remarks in a famous passage of *La Nausée*. I walk down the road, he says, my life is open before me. I do not know what will happen to me, and, if my life so far is anything to go by, nothing will. Even if something dramatic happens, if a car, say, runs me over and kills me, that will not have conferred meaning on a meaningless life, only brought it to an end. But if I open a novel and read in its first pages that the hero is walking down a deserted road I know that this is the beginning of an adventure, of love, perhaps, or espionage, it does not matter, it is an adventure. I feel the comforting thickness of the remainder of the novel between the thumb and index finger of my right hand and I settle back with satisfaction. This, after all, is why I am reading the novel in the first place. Not, as the banal view has it, in order to entertain myself, but to give myself the feeling that meaning exists in the world, even if *I* have not yet found it. That is the secret power of novels: they look like mirrors held up to the world, but what they are is machines that secrete spurious meaning into the world and so muddy the waters of genuine understanding of the human condition.

When Oliver Twist is taken into the house of the man whose pocket he has been wrongly accused of trying to pick, but who turns out to be surprisingly benevolent towards the wretched orphan, his eye is caught by a portrait hanging on the wall. 'Are you fond of pictures, dear?' asks the old housekeeper who is tending him. 'I don't quite know, ma'am', says Oliver, without taking his eyes from the canvass, 'I have seen so few that I hardly know. What a beautiful face that lady's is.' The housekeeper explains that it is a portrait, but that 'It's not a likeness of anybody that you or I know, I expect.' Nevertheless, Oliver is transfixed by it. 'The eyes', he says, as puzzled by his own reactions as is the old lady, 'the eyes look so sorrowful, and where I sit they seem fixed upon me. It makes my heart beat.' He adds in a low voice, 'as if it was alive and wanted to speak to me, but couldn't'. If this was a work by Poe we would know that this was a sign of the boy's madness or obsession and that the face in the portrait would turn out to be no-one's but his own. Dickens is altogether more benign. But perhaps that is the wrong way to describe the differ- ence. It is a question of attitude not to life but to narration. Poe seems driven by the need to make it clear that the coincidences in his plots do not spring out of the fabric of the world but only out of the head of his hero/narrator. In Dickens coincidence is that which oils the wheels of the plot. It is preposterous, when one comes to think about it, that the one gentleman the young thieves should pick on in the streets of London the first time they take Oliver with them should turn out to have a portrait of Oliver's aunt (for that is who she is), his dead father's sister, upon his walls, and preposterous that Oliver should immediately feel the affinity through the portrait. But it is necessary for the purpose of Dickens' plot, just as it is necessary that the one house Sikes decides to burgle, miles from London, should also turn out to have direct links with Oliver. Dickens senses this absurdity, and in the closing stages of the book, as the plot unravels, passes the responsibility on to Providence or God: 'When your brother', Mr Brownlow tells Monks, 'was cast in my way by a stronger hand than chance . . .' Of course it is nothing of the sort. It is the hands of no-one but Dickens himself that cast Oliver in Mr Brownlow's way. That, however, is something the form he has chosen can never admit. Whether this is merely a small example of bad faith which allows for a profound exploration of character and society, and so a price well worth paying, or whether the cost in terms of repression and falsification is simply too great, is a question each reader has to answer for himself.

Kleist, more aware than Dickens of what is at issue, ends *his* great novel, *Michael Kohlhaas* in a way that Poe, had he known of it, would have greatly admired. The eponymous hero, a righteous and law-abiding man, is so incensed at the way the authorities condone a blatant wrong perpetrated against him by an arrogant nobleman that he eventually takes the law into his own hands and ends up fighting the entire system, a fight that can only have one end: his own execution for the murder and pillage he has committed. He does, however, possess a piece of paper given to him by a gypsy woman, on which is written the fate of one of his tormentors, who is watching his execution. The man, moreover, is aware of this and is, we imagine, simply waiting for Kohlhaas's death to appropriate the document.

The Elector called out, 'Kohlhaas the horse dealer, now that satisfaction has been given you in this wise, you on your side prepare to satisfy His Majesty the Emperor, whose attorney stands right there, for breach of the public peace!' Taking off his hat and tossing it on the ground, Kohlhaas said he was ready to do so . . . He had just unknotted his neckerchief and opened his tunic when he gave a quick glance around the circle formed by the crowd and caught sight, a short way off, of the figure that he knew with the blue and white plumes, standing beween two knights whose bodies half hid him from view. Kohlhaas, striding up in front of the man with a suddenness that took his guard by surprise, drew out the capsule, removed the paper, unsealed it and read it through; and looking steadily at the man with the blue and white plumes, in whose breast fond hopes were already beginning to spring, he stuck the paper in his mouth and swallowed it. At this sight the man with the blue and white crest was seized by a fit and fell unconscious to the ground. Kohlhaas, however, while his dismayed companions bent over him and raised him from the ground, turned around to the scaffold where his head fell under the executioner's ax.

Kohlhaas swallowing the piece of paper with his enemy's fate inscribed upon it is Modernism's answer to the Victorian novel. *Michael Kohlhaas* was published in 1810.

We are now in a position to understand a little better the nature of the anxieties that gripped the writers of our opening examples. What is afflicting Mallarmé, Hofmannstahl, Kafka and Beckett is the sense that they feel impelled to write, this being the only way they know to be true to their own natures, yet at the same time they find that in doing so they are being false to the world – imposing a shape on it and giving it a meaning which it doesn't have – and thus, ultimately, being false to themselves. Their works feel like an interference with the world, as guilt-inducing as the boy's presence in the nut-grove in Wordsworth's poem: lacking proper authority they have strayed into a place where they should not be. Going back to the world of genres is not an option, any more than is a return to the world of the *ancien régime*. Hence Kafka's horrified confession to Brod: 'Literature helps me to live, but wouldn't it be truer to say that it furthers this sort of life?' and his aphorism: 'In your quarrel with the world, back the world.' Hence Beckett's talk of 'being weary of pretending to be able, of being able . . . of going a little further along a dreary road'. Hence the remark of Adrian Leverkühn, Mann's composer-hero: 'Why must it seem to me as if almost all, no all the means and contrivances of art *are good for parody only*?' In a world of geniuses but not apostles the very idea of a 'genius' has become nothing more than a sick joke.

The remarks of Kierkegaard and Sartre help explain why so many Modernist writers have been at pains to stress that their fictions are only fictions, not reality. Not in order to play games with the reader or to deny the reality of the world, as uncomprehending critics charge them, but, on the contrary, out of a profound sense that they will only be able to speak the truth about the world if the bad faith of the novel, its inevitable production of plot and meaning, is acknowledged and, somehow, 'placed'.

Here is Borges, for instance, on tigers: 'Never can my dreams engender the beast I long for', he writes. 'The tiger indeed appears, but stuffed or flimsy, or with impure variations of shape, or of an implausible size, or all too fleeting, or with a touch of the dog or the bird.' In the poem he devotes to the subject he ends: 'I go on/ Seeking through the afternoon time/ The other tiger, that which is not in verse.' 'To find the conclusion', said Kierkegaard, 'it is necessary first of all to observe that it is lacking, and then in turn to feel quite vividly the lack.'

Hamm, in Beckett's *Endgame*, is terrified by the sense that something nameless 'is taking its course', feels that 'something [is] dripping in my head . . . Splash, splash, always on the same spot.' 'Perhaps it's a little vein', he thinks. 'A little artery.' Then he pulls himself together: 'Enough of that, it's story time, where was I?' He ponders, then proceeds: 'The man came crawling towards me, on his belly. Pale, wonderfully pale and thin, he seemed on the point of – No, I've done that bit.' He resumes: 'I calmly filled my pipe – the meerschaum, lit it with . . . let us say a vesta, drew a few puffs.' But he can't go on with this farce, screams 'Aah' and berates himself: 'Well, what is it *you* want?' But nobody answers him and he has no option but to proceed: 'It was an extraordinarily bitter day, I remember, zero by the thermometer . . .' Later he tries out other versions: 'It was a glorious bright day, I remember, fifty by the heliometer . . .' and 'It was an exceedingly dry day, I remember, zero by the hygrometer. Ideal weather, for my lumbago . . .' 'I remember' is a sick joke, as much of an invention as the weather. Hamm remembers nothing, he only seeks through story-telling to understand what it is that is taking place. Story-telling, though, only seems to take him further and further away from any understanding of what it is that he really *wants*. What had seemed designed to help in the end only hinders.

As Kierkegaard understood, what *is*, the 'something' taking its course, belongs to a different order from what can be *imagined*. That is his perpetual gripe against Hegel, that he blurs the boundaries between imagination and reality to the detriment of both. 'Actuality cannot be conceived', he writes in his notebook.

> To conceive something is to dissolve actuality into *possibility* – but then it is impossible to conceive it, because conceiving something is transforming into possibility and so not holding on to it as actuality. . . But there's this deplorable confusion in that modern times have incorporated 'actuality' into logic and then, in distraction, forgotten that 'actuality' in logic is still only a 'thought actuality', i.e. possibility.

Not just in logic, not just in Hegel, but of course in the novel itself, the 'modern' form *par excellence*. That is what Beckett struggled with all his life. He dramatises it memorably in the best of his early stories, 'Dante and the Lobster'. Belaqua, the Dantesque hero of these stories, has, on his aunt's instructions, bought a lobster for her to cook for their dinner together. He watches in horror as she prepares to drop it into the boiling water. 'But it's not dead', he protests. 'You can't boil it like that.' She looks at him in astonishment:

> 'Have sense,' she said sharply, 'lobsters are always boiled alive. They must be.' She caught up the lobster and laid it on its back. It trembled. 'They feel nothing,' she said.
> In the depths of the sea it had crept into the cruel pot. For hours, in the midst of its enemies, it had breathed secretly . . . Now it was going alive into the scalding water. It had to. Take into the air my quiet breath.
> Belaqua looked at the old parchment of her face, grey in the dim kitchen.

'You make a fuss,' she said angrily, 'and upset me and then lash into it for your dinner.'

She lifted the lobster clear of the table. It had about thirty seconds to live.

Well, thought Belaqua, it's a quick death, God help us all.

It is not.

Beckett does all he can to put himself (and us) in the lobster's place. But of course he can never quite do so, because when we have finished the story we can put it down and turn to something else. The lobster, on the other hand, can only die, slowly. Is Belaqua, who senses this yet does nothing about it, more to be admired than his aunt? In a way, yes, in another, no. He is the archetypal liberal at whom every publisher targets a new book about the Holocaust or the Rwandan massacres or some other horror of our time. Beckett is sympathetic to him but is nevertheless appalled by this, and caps Belaqua's attempt to comfort himself with the thought that it's a quick death with the simple, emphatic phrase, delivered with all the authority he can muster, and knowing that it will acquire whatever authority a story can give by being placed at the very end: 'It is not.' But the phrase is of course still part of the story. Which means that, in Kierkegaard's formulation, we can imagine but not live it. It can make us imagine the lobster's agony, but by that very token we cannot *quite* imagine it. Even when a story is about the limits of the imagination, it is still calling on us to imagine. It has no other recourse. You can never succeed, for each time you think you have succeeded, each time the reader says: 'Ah, I see', you have failed. This was the rock against which Kierkegaard banged his head, again and again, as of course did Beckett, and Borges.

And that is why Modernists look with horror at the proliferation in modern culture of both fantasy and realism – both Tolkien and Graham Greene, as it were, both Philip Pullman and V.S. Naipaul. Not out of a Puritan disdain for the imagination or the craft of letters, but out of respect for the world. The two greatest post-war English novelists, William Golding and Muriel Spark, wrote out of this tension, and two of their finest works, *Pincher Martin* and *The Hothouse by the East River*, explore the issue head-on. Both novels deal with the desire we all have to cling to what we know and love best – ourselves. This deeply rooted and unconscious need to deny the fact of death, to deny our lack of control over our own lives, is equated in both works with the making of fiction.

In Golding's novel Pincher Martin, belying his given name of Christopher, the Christ-bearer, has been a deeply selfish man all his life – a man who does not recognise other people except as obstacles to his self-fulfilment. Now, shipwrecked on a rock in the middle of the ocean, he fights off the thought that the only thing that mattered to him, himself, is about to disappear by imagining a Robinson Crusoe-like act of survival on his island. But, as Muriel Spark says in *Memento Mori*, if you try to forget Death, he will remind you of his presence. The contours of the island have for some time been feeling vaguely familiar to Pincher Martin. Suddenly, with horror, he understands: the rock he has been climbing over has exactly the contours of his own tooth as his tongue slides over it in his mouth. What he had thought of as *in* the world *outside* him he suddenly understands to be a projection of his fevered imagination, basing itself on one of his own teeth. The extraordinary effect of this revelation on us as readers depends of course on the fact that we have been living every moment of his struggle to survive with Pincher Martin as we do with the heroes of all good novels. It would not work if we adopted a post-Modern insouciance in relation to the fictions we read. We live it then, but what Golding is telling us is that we live a kind of lie created to protect the inviolability of the self, even if it means the prodigious effort of imagining the entire world we live in. Pincher Martin, no less than Don Quixote, is the hero only of a novel he has created. And novels, Golding tells us, are projections of our imaginations on reality; but they are not meaningless projections. They have a purpose: to protect us from the reality of our deaths.

The moment of recognition in *Pincher Martin*, the moment when we grasp that what we had taken to be an adventure *in* the world is only (only?) a desperate mechanism by the psyche for survival at any cost, is one of the eeriest and most powerful moments in literature. Nothing in *The Hothouse by the East River* can match it. But that novel has its own strengths. We are in New York, where the radiators burn too hot and no-one knows any longer why they are alive. This is where the protagonists have ended up, after what we gather has been a full life. The book opens in a shoe-shop, with Elsa trying on a pair of shoes. Suddenly she has the impression that the salesman who is helping her is someone she has once known. She hurries out. Everywhere she goes people are startled by the fact that she casts her shadow in the opposite way to everyone else. Gradually the figures out of her past gather and the mystery of the shadow is explained. Elsa and her husband died many years before, in a train accident. They have, in a sense, only been kept conscious by their deep visceral determination to deny death, but here too the law holds that if you seek to deny him, Death will eventually remind you of his presence. As in the Golding, the novel itself comes to be seen as the result of that effort, and so its end signals the final release of those desperate souls into a kind of peace, the final defeat of the fevered imagination. Yet all this had itself to be imagined, as Wallace Stevens says. Imagination dead imagine, was how Beckett put it.

By an act of imagination and the mastery of their craft Golding and Spark, like Borges and Beckett, have escaped the strictures of Kierkegaard and Sartre. They have done so not, of course, because they wanted to be on the right side of eminent philosophers, but because, in a sense, their life depended on it. It is the same with all the Modernists, from Mallarmé to Kafka, from Virginia Woolf to Alain Robbe-Grillet. And there are, of course, as many ways of proceeding as there are artists. But the point is that, in a world without authority, each of them has to find his way for himself. No-one can do it for them. Each new attempt, as Eliot wrote in what could almost be described as a manual of Modernism, the *Four Quartets*,

> Is a new beginning, a raid on the inarticulate
> With shabby equipment always deteriorating
> In the general mess of imprecision of feeling,
> Undisciplined squads of emotion.

Always precise, though, he adds that we must not thereby be discouraged: 'For us, there is only the trying. The rest is not our business.'

7

The Marquise Went Out at Five

I have been talking about the classic novel as a lure and a temptation, to which the *real* writer, in Kierkegaard's terms, succumbs at his peril. I have been suggesting that because it subtly confuses possibility and actuality it produces in the reader the impression that he or she understands something – what it feels like to be a tiger, to be boiled alive as lobsters are – when full understanding is impossible and what the writer who cares for reality should be doing is making us grasp the distance that separates us from the tiger in his tigerness, the lobster dying. Further, since we cling to the belief that we ourselves will never die and use our imaginations to bolster that belief, the novel, the unfettered product of the imagination, actively prevents us from having a realistic attitude to ourselves and the world, and therefore from achieving any sort of firmly grounded happiness. Novels, in this analysis, are like drugs – a view Wordsworth seemed to have reached two centuries ago ('The invaluable works of our older writers', he writes in the Preface to the *Lyrical Ballads*, 'are driven into neglect by frantic novels, sickly and stupid German tragedies, and deluges of idle and extravagant stories in verse') and the sooner we are weaned off them the better.

But there are less apocalyptic reasons for feeling uneasy with the classical novel, for feeling that to write well one must somehow write *against* it. One of them is the sense of the novel's distance from gut feeling, and, linked to it, the sense of the arbitrariness of its plots. Holden Caulfield, in Salinger's *The Catcher in the Rye*, catches this brilliantly when he describes an English film he sees:

> Then he meets this nice, homey, sweet girl getting on a bus. Her goddam hat blows off and he catches it, and then they go

upstairs and sit down and start talking about Charles Dickens. He's both their favourite author and all. He's carrying this copy of *Oliver Twist* and so is she. I could have puked.

In his conversations with David Sylvester, Francis Bacon returns again and again to the contrast between what he calls 'illustration' and what he himself is trying to do. 'Is that what illustration means?' asks Sylvester, 'a kind of caution, a lack of relaxation?' 'Well,' answers Bacon, 'illustration surely means just illustrating the image before you, not inventing it. I don't know how I can say any more about it.' But he does say more in another conversation:

> When I was trying in despair the other day to paint that head of a specific person, I used a very big brush and a great deal of paint and I put it on very, very freely, and I simply didn't know in the end what I was doing, and suddenly this thing clicked, and became exactly like this image I was trying to record. But not out of any conscious will, nor was it anything to do with illus-trational painting. What has never yet been analysed is why this particular way of painting is more poignant than illustration. I suppose because it has a life completely of its own. It lives on its own like the image one's trying to trap; it lives on its own and therefore transfers the essence of the image more poignantly. So that the artist may be able to open up or rather, should I say, unlock the valves of feeling and therefore return the onlooker to life more violently.

'It lives on its own like the image one's trying to trap.' That is the key. That is what Wordsworth achieved in his greatest poems, what Rabelais and Cervantes, in their own ways, achieved. Illustration is accurate but dead. Bacon does not want to produce *an image* of what he has before him or in his mind, he wants in some sense to make what he does live a life of its own, just as what he has before him or in his mind lives its own life. He also, as he tells Sylvester, tends to prefer to paint one figure only because more than one leads to what he calls 'story-telling', the anecdotal, which is an extension of illustration: 'I think that the moment a number of figures become involved, you immediately come on to the story-telling aspect of the relationship between figures. And that immediately sets up a kind of narrative. I always hope to be able to make a great number of figures without a narrative.' 'As Cézanne does in the bathers?' asks Sylvester. And Bacon replies: 'Exactly.'

Yes, said Forster ruefully, novels tell stories. But, for the writer who feels as Bacon does, there must be ways of fighting this similar to Bacon's. First, as Kierkegaard said, it is necessary to feel that something is lacking and then to feel quite vividly the lack. In his great essay on reading Proust talks with what might seem surprising passion about the tyranny of the imperfect indicative, 'that cruel tense which portrays life to us as something at once ephemeral and passive, which, in the very act of retracing our actions, reduces them to an illusion, annihilating them in the past without leaving us, unlike the perfect tense, with the consolation of activity'. 'Even today', he adds,

> I can have been thinking calmly about death for hours; I need only open a volume of Sainte-Beuve's *Lundis* and alight, for example, on this sentence of Lamartine's (it concerns Mme d'Albany): 'Nothing about her at that time recalled [*rappelait*] . . . She was [*c'était*] a small woman . . . etc.' to feel myself at once invaded by a profound melancholy.

As so often, Roland Barthes merely develops the insights of the great Modernists, though with characteristic acuity. He discusses tenses in his first major work, *Le Degré zéro de l'écriture* (1953). It's perfectly possible, he points out, to write novels in the form of letters and to write history through analysis and economic tables, but at a particular moment, in the nineteenth century, both history and the novel chose as their preferred form what he calls the *récit*. And the keystone of the *récit* is the *passé simple*:

> Through its *passé simple* the verb implicitly takes its place in a causal chain, it participates in a group of actions which are of a piece and forward driven, it functions as the algebraic sign of an intention . . . It supposes a world which is constructed, elaborated, detached, reduced to a few significant lines, not a world which is thrown, displayed, offered [*jeté, étalé, offert*]. Behind the

passé simple there always hides a demiurge, god or reciter; the world is not inexplicable when one recites it . . . When the historian affirms that the duc de Guise died [*mourut*] on 23 December 1588, when the novelist recounts how the marquise went out [*sortit*] at five, these actions emerge from a past without density; freed of the trembling of existence [*du tremblement de l'existence*], they have the stability and the pattern of an algebra, they are a memory, but a useful memory, whose interest counts for much more than its duration.

. . . For all the great storytellers of the nineteenth century the world may be filled with pathos, but it is not abandoned, since it is a cluster of coherent relations, since there is no friction between the written elements, since he who recounts has the power to challenge the opacity and the solitude of the existences which make it up, since he can testify with each phrase to the possibility of communication and to a hierarchy of actions.

And he sums up:

The *passé simple* signifies a creation: that is, it signals it and imposes it. Even engaged in the most sober realism, it reassures, because, thanks to it, the verb expresses an act which is closed, definite, substantive. The *récit* has a name, it escapes the terror of a speech without limit. Reality grows thinner and becomes familiar.

Barthes' example of the marquise going out at five o'clock is a reference to a famous remark by Valéry, quoted by Breton in *The Surrealist Manifesto*, that the phrase was one he would always avoid, as it was the type of bad opening of classic nineteenth-century narratives. What Valéry hates about the phrase is its anecdotal character, what Bacon would call 'the story-telling aspect'. What Bacon and Valéry object to is the arbitrariness implied in the use of the phrase. The marquise went out at five o'clock, but why not at six or seven, and why a marquise and not a duchess? The classic novelist will reply: because in my story it's a marquise and she goes out at five, not six or seven. But there is something a little disingenuous in this. It's a marquise and not a duchess and she goes out at five and not six or seven because he has decided, for the purposes of his narrative, that this is how it will be. But the old question, raised already, we have seen, by Rabelais and Cervantes, still remains: What gives you the authority to decide that it will be this rather than that? No authority, the classic novelist will reply, but simply the requirements of realism, the requirements of my plot. But do these things have to do with anything other than ensuring that your novel is saleable? That of course is a very reasonable requirement, but let us then simply relegate it to the world of consumerism, of fitted kitchens and package holidays, and not pretend that we are dealing with aesthetic or ethical issues.

The problem, as always with the novel, is more complicated than either party quite realises. For when we talk about anecdotes, when we talk about what is arbitrary and what is necessary, we are not just talking about art, we are also talking about life. Kierkegaard and Sartre were right: we cannot hive off these problems as being merely problems of narrative. Narrative is so potent because telling stories is part of what being human is about. But that is all the more reason to be wary about how stories are told.

The way old Freddie told me the story it was as limpid as dammit. And what he thinks – and what I think too – is that it just shows what toys we are in the hands of Fate, if you know what I mean. I mean to say, it's no good worrying and trying to look ahead and plan and scheme and weigh your every action, if you follow me, because you never can tell when doing such-and-such won't make so-and-so happen – while, on the other hand, if you do so-and-so it may just as easily lead to such-and-such.

Life, P.G. Wodehouse's narrator suggests here, is all a matter of chance, or fate: I do so and so and such and such results, but I might well have done something slightly different and then something quite different would have resulted. But if life is like that can fiction afford to be? In fact it can't, or there would be no artefacts but an endless series of disorganised coincidences which would quickly bore the reader; yet it has to pretend it is doing just that if it is to retain the reader's belief that it is 'true to life'. Most novels are uneasy compromises between these two positions.

As always, what Modernism does is to drive the contradictions out into the open. In Borges' story, 'Death and the Compass', the dull police inspector, Treviranus, faced with a number of facts – a dead body in a hotel room, precious stones in the next room – comes up with the obvious explanation:

> 'No need to look for a three-legged cat here. We all know that the Tetrarch of Galilee owns the finest sapphires in the world. Someone, intending to steal them, must have broken in here by mistake, Yarmolinsky got up; the robber had to kill him. How does it sound to you?'

'Possible, but not interesting', replies the detective hero, Lonnröt.

> 'You'll reply that reality hasn't the least obligation to be interesting. I'll answer you that reality may avoid that obligation but that hypotheses may not. In the hypothesis you propose, chance intervenes copiously. Here we have a dead rabbi; I would prefer a purely rabbinical explanation, not the imaginary mischances of an imaginary robber.'

Lonnröt of course is right. He recognises that there is the banal reality of facts and probable causes and there is the aesthetic and existential need for pattern; the effort of the nineteenth-century novelist and historian to imply that the two are one does not hold up. But in Borges' brilliant story Lonnröt's intuition leads to his own demise, for the villain is, in this story, one step ahead of the detective. He has, in fact, produced an 'interesting' series of crimes precisely because he knows that Lonnröt has a weakness for the 'interesting', for the type of explanation in which chance is most fully eliminated. So, as a result of this, he ends up, like Oedipus, as the victim as well as the solver of the crime. But the ultimate victor is, of course, neither the villain nor the detective, but the story. Borges has succeeded in writing a story that avoids the vagaries of chance, the arbitrariness of Valéry's sentence about the marquise, that is as gripping as any detective story, and yet makes us recognise that it is human agency that is always at work.

It is precisely because Borges senses the world as 'thrown', 'offered', 'abandoned' (Barthes' surprisingly Heideggerian terms) and because for him, as for Proust and Kafka and Virginia Woolf, writing is a way of surviving in such a world, that he wages constant war on the classic tradition of fiction. In 'The Garden of Forking Paths' he imagines the answer to P.G. Wodehouse: a book in which the arbitrary would be abolished. In all books, he has a character here say, one incident leads on to another and the paths not taken are passed over in silence; but in the book of the Chinese ancestor of one of the two protagonists every possible forking of the paths is followed up and a garden of infinite paths is envisaged. It is envisaged in Borges' story, however, only in order to bring home to the reader *that which is other than all these forks*, the *now* in which a person, a flesh and blood individual, an 'existing individual', as Kierkegaard would say, meets his death: 'Then I reflected that everything happens to a man precisely, precisely *now*.'

Anecdotes, like the chain of past tenses of the classic novel, cannot ever convey that sense of 'the now', the sense that everything that happens to us happens precisely now. Anecdotes, rather, take us away from the now into a before and an after. In 'Tlön, Uqbar, Orbis Tertius', Borges approaches the problem in a different way. The narrator becomes aware of a purely imaginary world which is slowly encroaching upon our own, a world in which everything grows slender and pure and without density, in Barthes' words, a world frighteningly like the world of novels, but also like the one, the story suggests, which the Nazis tried to impose on our world in the years 1933 to 1945. In a very modern gesture of passive resistance or quiet heroism the narrator wages his own battle on this by retiring to a hotel by the sea to pursue, like a latter-day (stoical) St Jerome, his translation into Quevedian Spanish of Sir Thomas Browne's baroque masterpiece, *Urne Burial*. I say stoical because he is no longer confident that what he is doing is passing on the tradition, as St Jerome was doing. He has lost confidence in time. What he hopes for, simply, is that the quiet daily work of translation will keep *him* anchored to reality and prevent *his* being sucked into the seductive world of Tlön. That is the best that, in our modern world, we can hope for.

Borges' most famous story, 'Pierre Menard, Author of the Quixote', is his most ingenious, witty and melancholy exploration of these themes, with the quietly heroic narrator of 'Tlön, Uqbar, Orbis Tertius' turning into a demented Quixote- or Ahab-like artist determined to escape the Arbitrary and to find the

Necessary at any cost. A *fin de siècle* Symbolist writer devotes his life to rewriting *Don Quixote*, not in his own modern way but in Cervantes' way, that is, trying to feel himself into the *necessity* behind every arbitrary sentence of Cervantes. As always in the best of Borges the story is wonderful because it is so rich – not only is the central idea fascinating, but the world of hushed reverence he conjures up is both accurate and hilarious. 'It is a revelation to compare Menard's *Don Quixote* with Cervantes', says the awed narrator.

The latter, for example, wrote (part one chapter nine):

> . . . truth, whose mother is history, rival of time, depository of deeds, witness of the past, exemplar and adviser to the present, and the future's counselor.

Written in the seventeenth century, written by the 'lay genius' Cervantes, this enumeration is a mere rhetorical praise of history. Menard, on the other hand, writes:

> . . . truth, whose *mother* is history, rival of time, depository of deeds, witness of the past, exemplar and adviser to the present, and the future's counselor.

History, the *mother* of truth: the idea is astounding. Menard, a contemporary of William James, does not define history as an enquiry into reality but as its origin. Historical truth, for him, is not what has happened; it is what we judge to have happened. The final phrases – *exemplar and adviser to the present, and the future's counselor* – are brazenly pragmatic.

The contrast in style is also vivid. The archaic style of Menard – quite foreign, after all – suffers from a certain affectation. Not so that of his forerunner, who handles with ease the current Spanish of his time.

Any commentary on this would risk turning into another parody. So let the reader reread, and ponder.

Behind Pierre Menard, of course, stands the figure of Mallarmé, of all the nineteenth-century writers the one most obsessed with finding a way to write that would defeat the vagaries of chance. His mature poems are so difficult because his whole effort is directed towards creating a dense network of meanings or half-meanings, which emerge momentarily only to be overtaken by others as the syntax suddenly seems to deny the meaning one had been heading for. As one of his finest critics, Malcolm Bowie, puts it, 'each word is a gravitational centre around which possible meanings of the entire sentence gather'. He goes on, very finely: 'These virtualities will of course become fewer as we move towards a relatively stable syntactic armature for the poem. But the meanings we relinquish do not simply disappear: the atmosphere of multiple potentiality which they create is part of Mallarmé's substance.'

Here is one of Mallarmé's most famous poems:

> Le vierge, le vivace et le bel aujourd-hui
> Va-t-il nous déchirer avec un coup d'aile ivre
> Ce lac dur oublié que hante sous le givre
> Le transparent glacier des vols qui n'ont pas fui!
>
> Un cygne d'autrefois se souvient que c'est lui
> Magnifique mais qui sans espoir se délivre
> Pour n'avoir pas chanté la région où vivre
> Quand du stérile hiver a resplendi l'ennui.
>
> Tout son col secouera cette blanche agonie
> Par l'espace infligée à l'oiseau qui le nie,
> Mais non l'horreur du sol où le plumage est pris.
>
> Fantôme qu'à ce lieu son pur éclat assigne,
> Il s'immobilise au songe froid de mépris
> Que vêt parmi l'exil inutile le Cygne.
>   (a prose translation will be found in the notes)

The first thing to note is that this is clearly a sonnet. The second is that, unlike Baudelaire's poem on the swan, it does not have a title. The third is that, once one plunges into the poem one seems to find oneself in a labyrinth from which it is almost impossible to emerge. The first line is already rather odd, but anyone with even a little bit of French quickly realises that we are dealing with a subject, *aujourd'hui*, 'today', preceded by three adjectives. True, it is difficult to add these three together to create a full picture of the day, which is what we take to be the task of adjectives, for they seem to belong, somehow, to slightly different, overlapping worlds: *vierge*, 'virgin', suggests purity; *vivace*, 'vivacious', can, with an effort, be made to apply to an entity like the day, though it chimes oddly with *vierge*, even if linked to it by sound; while *bel*, 'beautiful', seems to us too bland to come as the climax of three adjectives, yet it again locks into the line acoustically. Even so, this is the end of any relative ease of response, for instead of the expected verb, *arriva*, 'arrived', perhaps (the day dawned), we have both a question, 'is it going to?' and an almost incomprehensibly violent action, *nous déchirer*, 'tear us', or 'tear for us', followed by a clause, 'with a drunken blow of wings' (meaning what?). Tear what? 'this hard lake forgotten' – but if it is forgotten, what kind of an object is it? And this in turn is qualified – the lake seems to be haunted, under its coat of hoar-frost, by the transparent ice of flights that have not taken place, of birds that have not flown away.

Our response to all this, as Bowie suggests, is either to try and get 'with panic-stricken rapidity' at 'what it means', or to abandon it for ever. 'The double effort required to allow Mallarmé's gaps their full disjunctive and destructive power', he says, 'yet at the same time remain attentive to the multitude of invisible currents which pass back and forth between the separated segments, will strike many readers as inexcusably arduous and unrewarding.' However, he concludes, 'the view I shall propose, is that . . . time spent learning to read Mallarmé is amply repaid'.

In a sense Mallarmé is only carrying to extremes what poetry has always done: playing off meaning against rhythm and rhyme, forward movement against stillness and repetition. English poetry contains many examples of dense and compacted poetry, often in the form of sonnets, from Shakespeare to Hopkins. We could say that what happens in such poems is that the clear distinction between foreground and background, between what the poet 'is saying' and 'how he says it', grows more and more blurred the more dense and compact the language. We can, in other words, after a while, provide a rough paraphrase of 'O the mind, mind has mountains; cliffs of fall/ Frightful, sheer, no-man-fathomed', but what Hopkins is saying cannot really be separated from how he is saying it. Or rather, to say the same thing in a different way would take several pages, while Hopkins does it in two lines. Those lines, moreover, are 'alive' in Bacon's sense, in a way the paraphrase would never be. Indeed, the poem as a whole fulfils Bacon's prescription for an art that is more than illustrational, anecdotal: 'It lives on its own, like the image one's trying to trap.' The reader engages with a living thing, not merely a 'story'.

Mallarmé's sonnet is less overtly dramatic than Hopkins', but it is just as 'alive'. Yet even here one firm foothold remains for the reader, in spite of the syntax, in spite of the dizzying negatives, and that is our knowledge, immediately acquired on first looking at it, that this is a poem, and that it is a sonnet. Even that assurance is removed, though, in the great work of Mallarmé's maturity, *Un Coup de dés*. As even those who have never read it know, Mallarmé, in that work, carried his explorations to an extreme by creating, for what he was trying to say, a form unlike any other, a form created to suit this work and no other.

The spatial disposition of the poem and its typographical distinctions bear little relation to the visual games played by Apollinaire or the use of Chinese ideograms by Pound in the *Cantos*. 'The space created by the poem', says Bowie, 'is for Mallarmé no more empty than physical space is for Descartes or for Einstein. It is rather a "field", a comprehensive realm of inter-related energies, which are organised yet indefinitely subject to mutation and inflection.' A central statement marches across this space: 'Un coup de dés jamais n'abolira le hasard', a throw of the dice will never eliminate chance. This is an odd statement in itself, since no-one ever imagined it could, but suggestive if we put it in the context of Kierkegaard's notion of 'the leap', a notion he toyed with all his life. By a leap the young man of *Either/Or* would become like the Judge; by a leap the anxious Christian like himself would become a Knight of Faith like Abraham. And just as Kierkegaard, writing about despair, realised that the only way to be true to his material was to work dialectically, so that he could explore the despair of necessity-without-possibility only by pairing it with the despair of possibility-without-necessity, so Mallarmé places around his mysterious central sentence a whole host of subordinate clauses, and clauses subordinate to those, and clauses hanging somehow on to those, and leaves it to us to decide how we want to make our way through his work, how many of the clauses we wish to take in, how many to ignore. As we move repeatedly through it we find ourselves in a world familiar to us from so much nineteenth- and twentieth-century writing: that of Kierkegaard, as I have said, but also that of parts of *The Prelude*, of Melville's *Moby Dick*, of Poe's *Arthur Gordon Pym*, of Mann's *The Magic Mountain*, a world of choice and necessity, of shipwreck and illumination, a world where the blank page or the whiteness of the whale or of snow is both the ultimate illumination and the ultimate disaster. It is also a world where distinctions between background and foreground have finally been all but abolished, where the white that surrounds the words is as meaningful as the words themselves, where sound, sight and meaning play with and against each other and are never allowed to settle. 'Tout se passe, par raccourci, en hypothèse; on évite le récit', said Mallarmé, with that wonderful down-to-earthness which is so endearing a trait of his character. That could of course be a description of any of his mature poems – 'Everything happens by means of short cuts, hypothetically; narrative is avoided' – but it applies most of all to this, his greatest poem.

Mallarmé is unique in the degree to which he pushed his explorations, but both his project and his execution of it help us to understand not only Modernist poetry but Modernism in general. 'Everything happens by means of short cuts, hypothetically; narrative is avoided' – that could be the prescription for a work that would overcome Valéry's strictures, Borges' dark forebodings. When Bowie remarks that 'these virtualities will of course become fewer as we move towards a relatively stable syntactic armature for the poem. But the meanings we relinquish do not simply disappear; the atmosphere of multiple potentiality which they create is part of Mallarmé's poetic substance', we cannot help thinking of the late novels of Henry James or the early novels of Alain Robbe-Grillet. 'Quite often the anecdotal details he has worked out in his plans do not merely disappear from the finished text but turn up as incidents he refers to as precisely what has not occurred', says Maurice Blanchot of James. 'Thus James experiences the negative of the story he has to write rather than the actual story', he adds. And he concludes his brief study of the novelist:

> What we might then call the passionate paradox of the plot in James is that it represents for him the security of a work

determined in advance, but also its opposite: the joy of creation, that which coincides with the pure *indeterminacy* of the work, which puts it to the test but without reducing it, without depriving it of all the possibles that it contains. And this is perhaps the essence of James's art: to make the whole work present at each moment, and even, behind the constructed and limited work which he brings into being, to allow us to feel other forms, the infinite yet weightless space of the narrative as it might have been, as it was before all beginnings.

And Blanchot notes that the name James himself gives to this gentle pressure on the work, 'not to restrict it, but on the contrary to extract everything from it so that it speaks without reticence while still maintaining its reticent privacy', is the same as the title he gave to his greatest story – 'the turn of the screw'. 'What then do I see my K.B. case [a plan for an unrealised novel] as yielding, once put under pressure and submitted to *the turn of the screw?*' (his italics) he writes in his Notebooks, showing that he was well aware of the real theme of his story, which is not the nature of ghosts or the innate evil of children or the fantasies of the housekeeper, but what happens when too much pressure is applied in order to force 'the truth' to be spoken, the 'reticent privacy' to be invaded.

Like James, Mallarmé's younger contemporary, Proust, is also concerned to escape from the thinness of the 'récit', its sad 'and then and then and then' quality, when 'doing such-and-such', in P.G. Wodehouse's terms, makes 'so-and-so happen'. Clearer sighted than James, Proust makes this the central motif of his novel from the very start. The opening meditation on sleep explains it all: a man, asleep, he tells us, is like a bundle of potential, every avenue open to him; even in the moments of going to sleep or waking up he still feels, floating around him, as it were, all the rooms he has inhabited and the women he has slept with. Once awake, however, he has to return to 'himself', to putting on 'his' clothes, to doing the things 'he' has to do that day, and so on. Yet the possible worlds hover like a halo round his head. He understands that his life has inevitably been conditioned, like all lives, by chance encounters, chance events. Swann, acquainted with Marcel's family because they have holiday homes in the same village, leads him to his daughter, Gilberte, and through her to the anguish of love and desire; but he also leads him to Bergotte and Balbec and Elstir and Albertine and all that subsequently unfolds in his life. Our existence is radically contingent. And yet the story of Swann himself, placed by the author near the start of his novel, demonstrates that despite the uniqueness and contingency of each of our lives, there are general laws of existence as well, which make us all behave in similar ways: the story of Swann's love for Odette parallels that of Marcel for Gilberte and then Albertine. At the same time the novel shows how it is possible to react to similar experiences in very different ways, to learn or not to learn from what one goes through. Swann, with that slight coarseness of spirit which characterises him, says Marcel, dismisses his affair with Odette with the remark: 'To think that I gave up the best years of my life to a woman who was not my type.' Marcel, on the other hand, more intelligent, more dogged perhaps in his desire to understand, comes to see that suffering and joy are not to be dismissed like that, but form part of the fabric of existence, the exploration of which becomes the theme of his life as a writer. All this makes nonsense of the claim, still sometimes heard, that Proust is merely the exquisite chronicler of the upper echelons of French society in the years leading up to 1914. He is no more that, just as James is no more that for English society, than either of them is like John Galsworthy or Roger Martin du Gard, writers who imagine that quality lies in the length of a work and in the number of generations it deals with. For both Proust and James, despite the length of their novels, the Mallarméan description holds good: 'Tout se passe, par raccourci, en hypothèse; on évite le récit.' And the work of both conforms to Bacon's recipe for a successful picture: 'It lives on its own, like the image one's trying to trap.'

8

A Universe for the First Time
Bereft of All Signposts

'This poem', Tolstoy wrote in *What is Art?* about Mallarmé's 'A la nue accablante tu', 'is not exceptional in its incomprehensibility. I have read several other poems by Mallarmé and they also had no meaning whatever.' Tolstoy was not alone in his suspicions, but neither was Mallarmé alone in being the subject of general incomprehension. In his early, rather romantic memoir-cum-meditation, *La Corde raide*, Claude Simon, who himself started out as an artist, describes a taciturn, friendless, obsessive painter, who also like himself had been born and bred in the South, returning day after day to the same spot, tramping over mountain and quarry, endlessly repeating the same motif, never satisfied, never stopping, his whole existence funnelled into the walk out to the mountain, and then the struggle to relate what he sees to what appears on his canvas until the light fades and he has to pack up his things and tramp home, unappeased, ready to start again the next day.

What is it that so obsesses him? That takes him from his family and friends into the same unyielding arena, day after day, with nothing but the mountain, the quarry, the trees and the sky, and that canvas rectangle on which he leaves his marks? Why is it that the paintings left by this man satisfy him, Simon, in a way no other artwork has ever done? Is it that while other paintings tell a story these seem to be alive? Is it the sense that everything on that canvas rectangle relates to everything else? That while never relinquishing the motif, Mont Saint-Victoire, the quarry at Bibémus, he reaches the point where, on his canvas, background and foreground cease to function as such and are replaced by a reticulation of painterly gestures with no slackness, no coasting, in any area? Talking later, Simon was to make just this point. Cézanne's mature work, he says, is characterised by a 'refus de valorisation sélective', a refusal to think of one element as more important than another: 'In his work the attention of the spectator is solicited by the whole surface', he says, 'and not only certain privileged spots or objects or people.'

Merleau-Ponty has unpacked for us what traditional landscape painting before Cézanne consisted of. When a painter is confronted by a landscape, he writes,

> he chooses to depict on his canvas an entirely conventional representation of what he sees. He sees a tree nearby, then he directs his gaze further into the distance, to the road, before finally looking to the horizon; the apparent dimensions of the other objects change each time he stares at a different point. On the canvas, he arranges things such that what he represents is no more than a compromise between these various different visual impressions: he strives to find a common denominator to all these perceptions by rendering each object not with the size, colours, and aspect it presents when the painter fixes it in his gaze, but rather with the conventional size and aspect that it would present in a gaze directed at a particular vanishing point on the horizon, a point in relation to which the landscape is then arranged along lines running from the painter to the horizon. Landscapes painted in this way have a peaceful look, an air of respectful decency, which comes of their being held beneath a gaze fixed at infinity. They remain at a distance and do not involve the viewer. They are polite company: the gaze passes without hindrance over a landscape which offers no resistance to this supremely easy movement.

It's amazing how close this description of traditional landscape – the pleasures it offers and the simplifications and distortions that entails – is to Barthes' description, quoted earlier, of the use of the *passé simple* in the traditional novel. And, as with the classic novel, this is not meant as an indictment of a whole tradition – we have seen Friedrich working very differently with landscape – but simply as a means of making us aware of the fact that what at first seems natural is actually highly artificial and constructed (one could make the same sort of analysis of the role of the key-system that underlies classical music). And, as Kierkegaard and Proust and Sartre noted with classic narrative, so here. 'This is not how the world appears when we encounter it in perception', Merleau-Ponty goes on:

> When our gaze travels over what lies before us, at every moment we are forced to adopt a certain point of view and these successive snapshots of any given area of the landscape cannot be superimposed one upon the other. It is only by interrupting the normal process of seeing that the painter succeeds in mastering the series of visual impressions and extracting a single unchanging landscape from them ... by subjecting all such details to this analytical vision he fashions on the canvas a representation of the landscape which does not correspond to any of the free visual impressions. This controls the movement of their unfolding yet also kills their trembling life.

Claude Simon, in *La Corde raide*, had made the same point, more dramatically. In Cézanne we see, he says,

> a universe for the first time bereft of all signposts, so totally bereft of everything except for truth and cohesion that for the first time it offered in its total magnificence, with neither commentary nor restriction, the visible world and, through it, the world itself ... It was something like the loss of all illusion. The loss of a dreamy and romantic virginity in exchange for a substantial knowledge, at once dazzled and disenchanted.

In traditional landscape the elements making up the scene – trees, hills, houses, sky – had been made visible, as it were, by being placed within a single perspective and given an outline, delineated. Cézanne came to understand, as he obsessively returned to his mountain, day after day, not only that nature does not conform to the laws of perspective set out in the manuals, but also that nature has no edges, that perspective and delineation are for the convenience of the artist who depicts it and the viewer who looks at it. But then what is to be seen? What is seeing itself? For Cézanne that mountain became what the white whale had been for Ahab, an element of the natural world which in time grew into a metaphysical obsession. How to capture it without humanising it, without turning it into an anecdote, 'that mountain which I, Cézanne, painted one day'? How, in Wallace Stevens's words, 'to see the earth again/ Cleared of its stubborn, man-locked set?' how, in Bacon's words, to give it a life on the canvas at least equal to the life it had in actuality? Partly this was a problem of seeing: how to see it as it is and not as I see it? And partly it was a problem of painting: how to mark the transitions from background to fore-ground, from that which surrounds a tree or mountain to the tree or mountain itself, since in nature there is no such thing as back-ground and foreground? 'We must render the image of what we see', Cézanne wrote to a young painter, 'forgetting everything that existed before us.'

Was it, like Ahab's quest, an ambition doomed to failure? Can any throw of the dice abolish the hazard of the contingent? Had not the traditional method of landscape in effect made the best of an impossible task? Perhaps so, but that did not satisfy Cézanne. And in the process of struggling, isolated and forgotten, with his demon, Cézanne produced a body of work which seemed to certain discerning artists who came after him and sensed what it was he was struggling with, to bring things to a new pitch. In his *Bathers* in the Barnes Collection, for example, the movements of the bathers seem, to Claude Simon, to have no discernible begin-ning or end: 'These almost asexual bodies in motion in an eternity without end and without any other reason than the radiant shim-mering of their gestures without beginning or end [*et sans autre raison que l'irradiant frémissement de leurs gestes sans commencement, sans fin*].' For Francis Bacon, as we have seen, they solved the problem of how to depict more than one figure yet not turn the painting into a story, an anecdote. At the same time, as Merleau-Ponty points out in his great essay, 'Le Doute de Cézanne':

It is Cézanne's genius that when the overall composition of the picture is seen globally, perspectival distortions are no longer visible in their own right but rather contribute, as they do in natural vision, to the impression of an emerging order, an object in the act of appearing, organising itself before our eyes [*d'un ordre naissant, d'un objet en train d'apparaître, en train de s'agglomérer sous nos yeux*]. In the same way, the contour of an object conceived as a line encircling the object belongs not to the visible world but to geometry. If one outlines the shape of an apple with a continuous line, one makes an object of the shape, whereas the contour is rather the ideal limit toward which the sides of the apple recede in depth. Not to indicate any shape would be to deprive the objects of their identity. To trace just a single outline sacrifices depth – that is, the dimension in which the thing is presented not as spread out before us but as an inexhaustible reality full of reserves [*non comme étalé devant nous, mais comme pleine de réserves et comme une réalité inépuisable*]. That is why Cézanne follows the swelling of the object in modulated colours and indicates several outlines in blue. Rebounding among these, one's glance captures a shape that emerges from among them all, just as it does in perception.

The agony for Cézanne, the doubt that he constantly feels about the value and even the point of what he is doing, stems from this, that he does not start with a given image, ready-made, but seeks instead to recreate each time the sense we have of the world coming to life as we look at it and live in it. As Merleau-Ponty says:

We live in the midst of man-made objects, among tools, in houses, streets, cities, and most of the time we see them only through the human actions which put them to use. We become used to thinking that all of this exists necessarily and unshakably. Cézanne's painting suspends these habits of thought and reveals the base of inhuman nature upon which man has installed himself. This is why Cézanne's people are strange, as if viewed by a creature of another species.

We have come across this sort of thing before, of course, in Wordsworth. But Wordsworth's intellectual error was to imagine that there was an earlier time *in life* when the world presented itself in this fashion, and he despaired of ever finding it again once he grew up. Merleau-Ponty's analysis of Cézanne suggests, rather, that this primal time is always there, waiting to be rediscovered by the artist. Of course there is no guarantee that it will be and no clear sense of what it is that is waiting to be rediscovered, but one thing is certain: it has to do with a dialogue between us and the world, a dialogue conducted through the medium of our art (the dialogue we saw taking place between the Boy of Winander and the owls and the poet and the boy). 'The painter', says Merleau-Ponty, concluding this part of his essay, 'recaptures and converts into visible objects what would, without him, remain walled up in the separate life of each consciousness: the vibration of appearance which is the cradle of things.'

Of course, as with Mallarmé, what Cézanne was doing was merely taking a little further what had been a key element in painting since its inception, though, as Bacon suggests in his conversations with David Sylvester, that had been partly hidden (perhaps fortunately, he says) by the many other functions which painting once had. But taking it further, which, to the artist himself, seemed the most natural thing in the world and indeed the only thing worth doing, led to accusations of wilful disregard of the public, to Tolstoy's dismissal of Mallarmé and to charges of deliberate uglification levelled at Cézanne. Ironically, today, over a hundred years after their work appeared, Mallarmé is still considered 'too difficult' even by those who make a habit of reading poetry, but reproductions of Cézanne hang on every student wall. One wonders which is the kinder fate.

Cézanne went on being an influence and an inspiration to Claude Simon for all his writing life, and it would be easy to show that his work takes after Cézanne in all sorts of ways: in the sweeping up of the torrent of history into a singular narrative with its singular, compulsive style, which colours the telling and what is told; in its refusal to grant any special status to human and especially moral sentiments, which makes *La Route des Flandres* in particular so great a war novel; in its ability to create worlds which feel both that they have always existed and that they are only present by virtue of the effort the narrator is making to speak. All this, of course, could also be seen as subscribing to the Mallarméan dictum: 'Everything happens by means of short cuts, hypothetically; narrative is avoided.' Which suggests that though there might be a particularly close bond between Simon and Cézanne, it is not so much direct influence we are talking about as the opening up of possibilities by early Modernists. So let us take another writer, very different from Claude Simon, much more sly, much sadder and more comic than him or than Cézanne and Mallarmé, but equally anxious to escape the arbitrariness of conventional narrative, its ready-made quality. Let us look at the opening page of Robert Pinget's 1969 novel, *Passacaille*:

Le calme. Le gris. De remous aucun. Quelque chose doit être cassé dans la mécanique mais rien ne transparait. La pendule est sur la cheminée, les aiguilles marquent l'heure.

Quelqu'un dans la pièce froide viendrait d'entrer, la maison était fermée, c'était l'hiver.

Le gris. Le calme. Se serait assis devant la table. Transi de froid, jusqu'à la tombée de la nuit.

C'était l'hiver, le jardin mort, la cour herbue. Il n'y aurait personne pendant des mois, tout est en ordre.

La route qui conduit jusque-là cotoie des champs où il n'y avait rien. Des corbeaux s'envolent ou des pies, on voit mal, la nuit va tomber.

La pendule sur la cheminée est en marbre noir, cadran cerclé d'or et de chiffres romains.

L'homme assis à cette table quelques heures avant retrouvé mort sur le fumier n'aurait pas été seul, une sentinelle veillait, un paysan sûr qui n'avait aperçu que le defunt un jour gris, froid, se serait approché de la fente du volet et l'aurait vu distinctement détraqué la pendule puis rester prostré sur sa chaise, les coudes sur la table, la tête dans les mains.

Comment se fier à ce murmure, l'oreille est en défaut.

(see notes for translation)

The first thing to say is how immediate and powerful the hold of the narrative voice is over us. The tone may be abrupt but we quickly adjust and actually take pleasure in filling in the gaps, trying to make sense of what is being said – for it is said in a tone which suggests authority. And yet that 'quelque chose' in the first paragraph is a little puzzling. Something must be broken – but what, and broken where? Ah, in 'la mécanique' – though nothing shows. It must be the clock that is being talked about. But why 'must be broken' if nothing shows? The next sentence is a little odd again, for it is in the conditional – 'viendrait d'entrer' instead of 'venait' or 'vient' – '*would have* come in'. However, we read on. This person has sat down at the table. It is winter. All is in order. Again, as with the broken clock, there is something a little in excess of mere description here, but we can't quite pin it down. Suddenly, though, while the calm narrative tone persists, everything seems to speed up. 'L'homme assis à cette table quelques heures avant retrouvé mort sur le fumier' is ambiguous: was the man now sitting at the table found dead a few hours earlier on the dung-heap (and how could he then be sitting at the table?), or was the man sitting at the table a few hours earlier later found dead on the dung-heap? Barbara Wright, Pinget's wonderful English translator, opts for the latter reading, as being the less absurd, but the point is that in the French we feel a sudden lurch as time is compressed, bewilderingly, though again the narrator seems unaware of this but simply proceeds to point out that the man was not alone ('would not have been alone') in the room. He was, we are told, being spied upon by someone at the window, who *would have seen him* dismantling the mechanism of the clock and then sitting again at the table, head in hands. Again the narrative makes a leap, so that we are no longer sure who is speaking or about what: 'how to trust this voice, the ear is not up to it'.

The narrative is both much slower and much faster than in a traditional novel. Like a piece of music by Birtwistle it spirals forward via repetitions which are never quite repetitions, until we find ourselves in possession of far more information than would have been the case in a conventional narrative or symphony. We have a man alone in a room, sitting at a table, his head in his hands; a clock that may or may not have been interfered with; a corpse on a dung-heap; a watcher at the window. All this would seem to suggest a detective or murder story, but it clearly is not a detective story of the usual type. There is this insistent counterpoint to the detail: 'something broken in the mechanism but nothing shows'; 'how to trust this voice, the ear is not up to it'. The mechanism may be the clock, but it may also be the story itself, which someone is trying to tell, and which is both beautifully lucid and full of gaps and even contradictions. Can we make sense of it by latching on to that last phrase and saying: Ah, it's a story about someone (mis)hearing a story? But that doesn't quite work either, for this hypothetical protagonist never materialises, remains, like everything else here, merely latent, 'hypothetical'. The narrative goes calmly on its odd way, as more and more elements are dropped in, elements which have to do with a possible murder in the depths of rural France, with the backbiting and spying endemic to all village communities, but also with the broken-down mechanism and the unreliable ear, with solitude and desolation and loss. It is, we remember, called *Passacaglia*, and the musical title is perhaps the one we have to focus on, for, as we read, the narrative generates a sonorous, distinctive music, based, like all baroque music, on repetition and dance. It leaves one, as one finishes it, with the sense of having lived through half a dozen or more potential novels: Simenon-like novels about murder in the rural hinterlands of France, Mauriac-like novels about petty jealousies behind tightly shut windows, Proust-like novels about authors in search of their subjects; of having lived through them or half lived through them, and through so much else – child murder, desperate solitude, the system by and for which one has lived slowly collapsing round and perhaps even within one. But more than that, the book leaves one with the sense of having participated in the birth of narrative itself. And, naturally, having no beginning, the book has no end, no third part, as Kierkegaard would say. When the field has been thoroughly tilled the book stops, for nothing more can or needs to be said.

Our response to it, or to the novels of Claude Simon or Alain Robbe-Grillet, particularly if we have been brought up on a diet of Angus Wilson and Iris Murdoch, of Philip Roth and Toni Morrison, is likely to be precisely that which Malcolm Bowie posited of the reader of a Mallarmé poem: either to try to get 'with panic-stricken rapidity' at 'what it means', or to abandon it for ever. 'The double effort required to allow Mallarmé's gaps their full disjunctive power', we recall Bowie saying, 'yet at the same time remain attentive to the multitude of invisible currents which pass back and forth between the separated segments, will strike many readers as inexcusably arduous and unrewarding.' Yet, he concludes, 'the view I shall propose is that time spent learning to read Mallarmé is amply repaid.' I would only add that Bowie is perhaps a little too defensive, or at least that reading Pinget, Simon or Robbe-Grillet is infinitely easier than reading Mallarmé, and that it is exhilarating rather than arduous. But then I imagine Bowie really believes this holds true for Mallarmé as well.

9

The Mutilated Body Was Thrown Back Into The Sea

Here is a cultural historian's view of Cubism:

> For centuries painters had faced the task of providing an illusion
> of three-dimensionality in a two-dimensional medium . . . Now
> the first Cubists . . . Pablo Picasso and Georges Braque, rejected
> these time-honoured solutions: they were intent on making
> works of art that would not let the viewer forget their distinct
> essence as human products. They shattered surfaces that in
> nature belong together and reassembled fragmented reality by
> transforming a curved object like a woman's breast or a man's
> cheek into some strange geometric contour that resembled
> virtually nothing, certainly not a breast or a cheek . . . After the
> austerity of the founding years, the time of analytic Cubism,
> its successor, Synthetic Cubism, worked with a brighter palette
> and its canvases intensified their alienation from nature with
> stencilled inscriptions and arbitrarily added pieces of paper.

What Barthes said about the classic novel and Merleau-Ponty about
the classic landscape applies to this bit of prose. The story moves
forward in its inevitable progression, imparting information evenly
and calmly: 'the first Cubists . . . They shattered surfaces . . . After
the austerity . . .' Nothing is at stake here, nothing signals to us that
at every moment choices were being made, decisions taken, lives
being ruined or saved. And I am not talking about a more biogra-
phical approach being needed, only an awareness that living and
telling are not the same thing at all, and that though we, as readers
and viewers looking back, inevitably lack the sense of what it was
like to live certain moments, the historian can work to counter that,

as indeed the best ones do, and, when dealing with works of art we can, if we are good enough critics, get close enough to them to convey something of what their making involved for their makers and first viewers.

Such a critic is Rosalind Krauss. Here is the start of her remarkable long essay on the series of little collages Picasso made between the autumn of 1912 and the spring of 1913, as he was gradually emerging from his passionate involvement with Cubism:

> At first they seem to rotate through the crystalline atmosphere like so many weightless facets, the glittering light of an invisible gem. Now one of the fragments appears aqueous, like water beading the side of a bottle; now it dries to the shimmer of dust motes struck by a ray of sunlight . . .
>
> But then there arises the sound of voices. They speak of a political meeting, of market shares. Someone tells of a woman who poisoned her lover, 'A chauffeur kills his wife,' says another. Who says? Whose voice? . . .

Though she does not say so in so many words, Krauss sees these collages as constituting as remarkable a series as any in the artist's oeuvre, and as marking a crucial moment in Modernist art. But she senses that, if she is to open our eyes so that we can see what she sees, she will have to work from the inside, not merely repeat the clichés of previous commentators.

The voices she is talking about are those that spring out of the fragments of newspaper the artist has cut up to use in these works. Scholars have recently begun to read these as well as seeing the shapes that have been made out of them, and have come up with fascinating facts. Picasso made great use of articles on the looming Balkan wars ('Les Alliés signent l'Armistice. La Grèce s'abstient'), as well as of the kind of *faits-divers* Félix Fénéon used in his delightful *Nouvelles en trois lignes* ('In Fontainebleau a tramp turns himself in for murder'), the financial news, and advertisements for everything from biscuits to massage parlours. He also, and more obviously, cut up headlines to provide witty allusions, 'Un Coup de Théatre', for example, becoming 'Un Coup de Thé', not only a (sort of) cup of tea but an allusion to Mallarmé's great poem, recently published in its correct format.

How are we to read these fragments? Who, as Krauss puts it, is talking? Some scholars have argued that they reflect Picasso's own anarchist, left-leaning views: 'The news items accumulate', Krauss quotes Patricia Leighton as saying, 'to project an image of French politics as venal, power-mongering, and posing a crazy threat to all those values of humanity and civilisation that Picasso's work had always embraced.' Others say that we are required simply to get the 'feel' of the different voices, not to decode them, that they represent Picasso and his friends sitting round a café table (the objects depicted in these collages are, apart from the musical instruments, the common furniture of the café tables of the time: glass and jug, bottle, newspaper, etc.) and talking endlessly about politics and life.

And what of the visual look of these little collages? Writing about *Violin* of autumn 1912 (*figure 4*), Krauss points out that 'One of the fragments of newspaper is the other's twin – having originally been scissored from the same sheet, so that, as in a jigsaw puzzle, both match along their common edge – only now flipped relative to the other, back to front.' She goes on to demonstrate how Picasso conjures the violin into life and how he forces us to work to keep up with him. One of the pair of cut-outs, she argues, the lower one, 'exploits the scrollwork of its left-hand edge to assume the profile of a violin. Or rather half a violin, since it depends on Picasso's drawn addition of bridge and neck and right-hand side to elaborate the musical instrument.' The other fragment of newsprint, 'placed above the violin's shoulders, deploys its own notches and curves to cup the pegs and scroll of the instrument, becoming thus their "background". In this position the lines of type now assume the look of stippled flecks of graphite.' Thus, she goes on, where the first fragment produced the meaning: density and opacity of physical object, this one 'summons forth a different sign. *Light*, it declares, or *atmosphere*'.

But Krauss has not finished. The magic of the whole collage, she suggests, rests on the fact that the two opposite meanings, light and opacity, are generated from the identical scrap of paper, the same physical shape. 'Like Saussure's phonetic substance', she says,

> this support is seen to take on meaning only within the set of
> oppositions that pits one against another, the implosive *p* of *up*

figure 4 Pablo Picasso, *Violin*, Autumn 1912. Pasted paper and charcoal on paper.

against the explosive *p* of *put*. Picasso's sheet, sliced in two, is thus a paradigm, a binary couple married in opposition, each taking on a meaning insofar as it is *not* the other. *Figure* and *ground* become this kind of contrary here, joined and redoubled by *opaque* and *transparent* or *solid* and *luminous*, so that just as one fragment is, literally speaking, the back side of the material from which the other was cut, the circulation of the sign produces this very same condition, but semiologically, at the level of the sign: *front, solid, shape: behind, transparent, surround.*

And she goes on to draw a general conclusion:

Does [Picasso] need to declare any more forcefully that here, in the fall of 1912, with his new medium of collage, he has entered a space in which the sign has slipped away from the fixity of what the semiologist would call an iconic condition – that of resemblance – to assume the ceaseless play of meaning open to the symbol, which is to say, language's unmotivated, conventional sign?

What is particularly witty about this example is that in a sense the whole thing is done by means of the two *f*-holes of the instrument – 'the fortuitous lettering offered up to him by the real', as Krauss puts it – since he places one, very large, in opposition to the other, very small, inscribing them onto a flat surface that squarely faces the viewer:

It is their unequal size that then acts on this frontality, as it produces the sign for foreshortening, for the swivelling of the object into depth, like a door that is slowly swinging open. Scripting the *f*s onto the face of the violin, where manifestly there is nothing but flatness, Picasso writes *depth* onto an object set squarely before us and only as deep as a sheet of paper. 'Depth', he says [. . .]

How does this depth relate to the 'depth' of the voices that have been speaking out of the newsprint itself? And how are we to take all these voices? To answer this Krauss turns to Bakhtin and to his comments on the multiple voices in a Dostoevsky novel. Bakhtin argues in his book on Dostoevsky that we are faced here with a wholly new kind of novel, a polyphonic work in which multiple voices make themselves heard. Every thought, he says, 'senses itself to be from the very beginning a *rejoinder* in an unfinalized dialogue. Such thought is not impelled toward a well-rounded, finalized, systemically monologic whole. It lives a tense life on the borders of someone else's thought.' But, as Bakhtin himself realises, it is easy to pay lip service to such an insight only to reduce the novel once again to monologue in one's mind (remember Kierkegaard on the difficulties of true negative thinking). One way of doing this

> is to take the polyphony present in the novels as a reflection of the multivoicedness found in the real world and thus 'to transfer [one's] explanations directly from the plane of the novel to the plane of reality.' The effect of doing this . . . is to characterize the novel as a single consciousness's vision of this fragmented world, something that is quite the contrary of Dostoevsky's procedure.

The other is 'to understand the constant voicing of different positions as part of an ideological project and to try to identify which of these ideas is Dostoevsky's own'. The equivalent positions in relation to Picasso's collages are the ones that take them as representing the group of left-leaning friends talking round the coffee-table, and those that see them as projecting Picasso's own theory of newspapers as secret instruments for perpetuating the status quo. But both these are false conclusions, both deny the radical multivoicedness of Picasso's collage.

Though Bakhtin is helpful to Krauss at this juncture in her argument, I am not convinced that he quite makes the case he is trying to make for Dostoevsky. A reader of Krauss who had grown up with Eliot and Virginia Woolf, however, would have no difficulty in seeing what she was trying to do. Eliot himself, of course, tries to 're-monologise' *The Waste Land* by suggesting, in his notes, that all that we are reading happens in the head of one of the characters mentioned in it, Tiresias; and there have been countless analyses of the poem which argue that what it 'depicts' is the fragmentation consequent upon the First World War. But Eliot's poem works precisely in the way Krauss suggests Picasso's collages do, and that

the poet himself sensed this is suggested by the epigraph he originally intended to append to the poem, from Dickens: 'He do the
police in different voices.' In the event he came upon something
better, an epigraph that can and cannot be read (rather as the
smaller fragments of type in Picasso's collages can and cannot be
read: you need a magnifying glass), since it is in a mixture of Latin
and Greek, and thus plays with the reader in the same way as do the
other quotations and fragments of other languages embedded in
the poem; for, deciphered, it touches on a central theme of the
poem, death-in-life, but *decipherment* is also one of the key issues
raised by the poem. The poem, like the 1912 *Violin*, flies off in
different directions and slyly plays at the border between figure and
ground, between our sense of incomprehension and our awareness
that there is comprehension, but, to paraphrase Kafka, not for us.

To reconstitute the fragments is, in Kierkegaard's terms, to turn
what is lived experience into thought experience, whereas both
collage and poem explore what happens precisely when the one is
turned into the other. The modern waste land, as Eliot describes
it, is a place where thought and naked desire have taken the place
of feeling and comprehension, which have almost completely
atrophied. This situation, as we have already seen, is difficult to
grasp precisely because to 'grasp' it is already to have lost it, to
have become like the characters in all Eliot's early poems who can
only think, not feel, who know too much but understand nothing.

A beautiful essay by John Mepham on Virginia Woolf's *To the
Lighthouse* can help us in our own quest to understand. In Part III
of the novel Lily Briscoe stands looking out to sea, painting and
letting her mind wander over the past and especially over the
presiding angel of the house, Mrs Ramsay, now dead, as she
watches the boat carrying Mr Ramsay and his two children being
rowed across the bay by the fisherman's boy. Suddenly (we are at
the end of section 5) she finds there are hot tears in her eyes:

> Was she crying then for Mrs Ramsay, without being aware of
> any unhappiness? . . . What was it then? What did it mean?
> Could things thrust their hands up and grip one; could the blade
> cut; the fist grasp? Was there no safety? No learning by heart
> of the ways of the world? . . . 'Mrs Ramsay!' she cried aloud.
> 'Mrs Ramsay!' The tears ran down her face.

6

[Macalister's boy took one of the fish and cut a square out of its side to bait his hook with. The mutilated body (it was alive still) was thrown back into the sea.]

7

'Mrs Ramsay!' Lily cried, 'Mrs Ramsay!' But nothing happened. The pain increased. That anguish could reduce one to such a pitch of imbecility, she thought! . . . Heaven be praised, no-one had heard her cry that ignominious cry, stop pain stop! . . . No-one had seen her step off her strip of board into the waters of annihilation. She remained a skimpy old maid, holding a paint-brush on the lawn.

And now slowly the pain of the want and the bitter anger (to be called back, just as she thought she would never feel sorrow for Mrs Ramsay again . . .) lessened; and of their anguish left, as antidote, a relief that was balm in itself, and also, but more mysteriously, a sense of someone out there, of Mrs Ramsay, relieved for a moment of the weight that the world had put on her, staying lightly by her side . . .

Why does Virginia Woolf introduce Macalister's boy at this point? Why interrupt our communion with Lily in her moment of anguish? For that interruption is no simple Brechtian alienation, it is a wrench, a tearing at the fabric of our being, quite as powerful in its way as Lily's sudden and unexpected experience of the death of Mrs Ramsay.

'To find the conclusion it is necessary first of all to observe that it is lacking and then in turn to feel quite vividly the lack of it.' In Part II of the novel Virginia Woolf had already begun to make us feel the lack when she killed off Mrs Ramsay in a bracketed aside. That's how it is, she seems to be saying, that's how loss occurs, unexpectedly, often very quickly, and how do we come to terms with the pain? There, as Mepham notes, she had used round brackets. Now she interrupts our communion with Lily's anguish with a whole new section, set in remorseless square brackets, and the effect is to make us experience, against our will, the fact that the world consists of more than our sorrows and joys; that many things go on simultaneously; that there is Lily Briscoe engaged with her painting; that there is the journey (at last) of the children to the lighthouse; that there is the daily life of the sea for Macalister's boy; that there is a dreadful death for the fish, mutilated and bleeding, and thrown without a thought back into the sea. This does not mean that Lily's loss is any the less real; but then neither is the excitement of the children nor the pain of the fish. All form part of the fabric of a larger life, fragments of a whole that must be accepted as beyond our imaginative grasp. And, as Kierkegaard understood, it is only with this almost unbearable realisation (realisation is hardly the word, this is something we experience viscerally or not at all) that some sort of healing can occur: the anguish lessens and leaves a sense of relief 'that was balm in itself'; but also, 'more mysteriously, a sense of someone out there, of Mrs Ramsay, relieved for a moment of the weight that the world had put on her, staying lightly by her side . . .'

There is no talk of redemption here, or even of understanding. Just as in *The Waste Land* the thunder gives a hint of rain to come but no more, though the *poem*, having exhausted itself, so to speak, ends in the quiet threefold repetition of that mysterious word, so soothing to pronounce: *shantih, shantih, shantih*. In both works, as in the majority of Modernist works, something happens as it unfolds, but it does not happen so much to the characters (though in a novel like *To the Lighthouse* there may be one especially privileged character, a sort of proxy of the author, such as Lily Briscoe) as to the reader (and to the author as reader of his or her own work). All we can say is *that something has become unblocked, a change has taken place.*

'Building a modern imperial capital', writes Robert Gildea about mid-nineteenth-century Paris,

> meant piercing broad boulevards, cutting long perspectives from one grand monument to the next . . . increasing the number of avenues radiating from the Étoile from five to twelve . . . and redesigning the Bois de Boulogne to include lakes, gardens, two race-courses and a zoo. In the railway age that was now reaching its apogee it meant driving arterial roads

to the main termini, from which railways fanned out to every part of France. 'Everything moves towards Paris: main roads, railways, telegraphs,' Haussmann announced in 1859, 'everything moves out from it: laws, decrees, decisions, orders, officials.'

The modern capital is thus both like the classic novel itself and the place of entertainment and leisure where such works are to be consumed; and if not on a bench in the Bois de Boulogne then on one of the trains carrying the eager visitor to the capital or taking the weary inhabitant of the city on holiday to one of the far-flung parts of the country now so easy to reach.

In 1967 Marguerite Duras published a novel which almost seems to have been written to challenge Haussmann's confident imperialism. *L'Amante anglaise* deals with a crime, and, to that extent, is precisely the sort of book you would read on a train. But the crime it deals with and the manner in which it deals with it make it the very opposite of a detective story.

A murder has been committed: dismembered portions of a body, but not the head, have been turning up in the open carriages of freight trains all over France. By a brilliant piece of deduction, the police work out that there is only one spot in France through which all the trains have passed, a viaduct in the village of Viorne on the western outskirts of Paris. The book begins with the arrival in a local café of a police inspector and his (female) assistant, in plain clothes, a few days after notices have been posted in the village asking the inhabitants to report anything suspicious to the police, especially the mysterious disappearance of a friend, neighbour or lodger. The book consists of three sets of taped interviews, the first with the proprietor of the café, Robert Lamy (and into this has been inserted the tape that was secretly running in the policeman's briefcase, and recording the opening scene), the second and third with a couple, Pierre and Claire Lannes, who were in the café that evening. The interviews are conducted, after the case has been solved, by someone who appears to be an investigative journalist of sorts, a kind of Truman Capote or Norman Mailer. Unlike his American counterparts, however, he does not figure in the book except as the person who (we understand) sets up the tape machine and asks the questions. We as readers are only given what is said on the tapes. This is frustrating, for what is the point of a murder mystery without background and explanations and conclusions, but also exhilarating as it is we, like everyone else involved, who have to make up our own minds, only given words to work with. The investigator sets things in motion with a comment of his own which is duly recorded: 'All that is said here is recorded. A book about the crime of Viorne begins to unfold. (*Un livre sur le crime de Viorne commence à se faire*.)'

In the first interview Robert Lamy tells how they heard about the crime; how naturally everyone was talking about it; how that evening Pierre and Claire came in with their friend Alfonso, a Portuguese odd-job man; how the stranger and the girl joined in the conversation and were quickly identified as the police; how the policeman explained that since no-one had come forward to report anyone missing the victim must have been a close member of a family or a friend; and how, as the policeman went on to reconstruct the events and to suggest that the body must have been cut up in the forest, Claire, who had been silent throughout, suddenly interrupted him and said that, no, it had been cut up in the cellar. She then confessed everything, Lamy says: she was the culprit, the victim was her cousin, Marie-Thérèse, a deaf-mute who lived with them and looked after the house, and who, she had told her husband, had returned for a while to her native Cahors.

'I'm trying to understand who this woman, Claire Lannes, is and why she says she committed the crime', says the interviewer to Robert, towards the end of the interview with him. 'She gives no reason for the crime. So I am looking for a reason for her.' Motive had already been discussed before Claire confessed. The policeman says, 'it seems to me that here one person killed another as they might have killed themselves (*il me semble qu'ici on a tué l'autre comme on se serait tué soi*) . . . It's what often happens, you know.' 'Because they loathed themselves or the other?' 'Not necessarily . . . Because they were together in a situation that had gone on for too long, not an unhappy situation, you understand, but fixed, without issue.' The interview with the husband yields nothing further: he had once loved his wife but she had grown absent, strange, a little mad. He didn't feel she even noticed him any more. She was fond of her cousin, he thought. She liked sitting in the garden for hours at a time on a bench by the English mint, *la menthe anglaise*. At one time she wrote letters to the papers. She wrote about the mint. She spelt it 'L'amante en glaise'. 'Perhaps the minute before she killed her she had no idea she was going to do it. Don't you think?' When the interviewer asks him who his wife was, he says: 'I don't know.' 'Think', says the interviewer. 'I don't want to', he says. 'One can explain everything if one wants to, or nothing, as one likes. So I'm keeping my mouth shut.'

Any thought that Claire will provide the explanation is soon dispelled. She has, she says at once, told the magistrate everything. She hasn't got an answer to the question of why she did it. It's not the right question. 'If they'd found the right question to ask me', she says, 'I'd have said. If I'd found the right question.' One thing, though: she refuses to say where the head is. She found Marie-Thérèse's rich meat sauces nauseating, she says. The mint in the garden was the opposite to those meat sauces. 'Sitting by that plant I was intelligent,' she says. 'Now I'm just me, but there . . . I was what remains after my death.'

So the criminal is found. Haussmann was right: the law at the centre can now reach out to any part of France, no matter how hidden. But the head of the victim has not been found and the question of why the murder was committed or who Claire Lannes is has not been answered. Yet this is not felt as a loss by the reader. On the contrary. The constant circling round the event and the refusal to come up with explanations convey a far more powerful sense of 'what happened' than Capote or Mailer ever manage. Above all the primacy of the event, the way it transcends all motive, all explanation, is borne in on us. In this it is like Greek tragedy; Claire, like Oedipus, we feel, is polluted but not guilty. To try and grasp what this means we go back to the beginning and start to read again: '*Un livre sur le crime de Viorne commence à se faire.*'

When Mallarmé said that he felt stupefied, nullified, by the effort of writing, and on top of that disgusted with himself; when Hofmannsthal's Lord Chandos said that he had lost the ability to speak in a coherent fashion; when Kafka lamented that he hadn't written a single line that he could accept, that his body put him on his guard against every word; and Beckett that he was weary of going a little further along a dreary road – they all testified to their revulsion at having, for the sake of something called art, to repeat the confused and half-thought-through actions of their predecessors, which, far from shedding light on the human condition, only muddied the waters. When Lord Chandos confessed to being moved only by the unnamed or the barely nameable, an abandoned harrow, a dog in the sun, a cripple, he touched unwittingly on the antidote to this, the effort, through art, to recognise that which will fit into no system, no story, that which resolutely refuses to be turned into art. That effort is at the heart of the Modernist enterprise.

10

Fernande Has Left With A Futurist

What Rosalind Krauss discerns as happening in the Picasso collages of 1912–13 is a key moment in Modernism's understanding of itself, not just a moment in Picasso's personal odyssey. For it is the moment when artists grasped that what they were producing were signs or emblems for the external world, not mirrors reflecting it. With that insight, however, as Rosalind Krauss realises, a new abyss yawned: is art then nothing but the circulation of signs?

Picasso's hatred of Futurism and of abstraction is well documented. As always with these things motives are mixed and strongly held views overdetermined. Krauss quotes a letter from Picasso to Braque in May 1912: 'Fernande has left with a Futurist. What am I going to do with the dog?' But, as she shows, personal pique connected with his loves, wounded pride at feeling that he, the torchbearer of the Modern, was being outflanked on two sides and starting to look distinctly *vieux jeu*, and a deeper, more purely artistic instinct, all played their part. 'The avant-garde had moved on in the early teens and was now lying in wait for cubism', she writes. 'It had other tricks up its sleeve, not the least of which was pure abstraction on the one hand and the photomechanical conception of art – in which the readymade combines with the photograph – on the other.' But Picasso clearly loathed the idea that Cubism should be thought of as 'non-objective art', just as he hated the notion that it had opened the way for the mechanical strategy of the readymade as Duchamp and Picabia were busy developing it.

Picasso turned his back on both abstraction and the mechanical, returned to his study of late Cézanne, and began, in the years that followed, to move towards what came to be called Neoclassicism. His disciples never forgave him. It was in those years, 1915–20, that the label of *pasticheur*, which has clung to him ever since, was first attached to him. Marinetti, Picabia, Rodchenko, Malevich, Mondrian – they were the purists, who saw how things were and drew their stern conclusions. Picasso seemed to be lost in a venture that was at once bourgeois and retrograde, suggesting in retrospect that even in Cubism, the one 'movement' he claimed all his life to have been *his* invention, he was only imitating others, in this case Braque.

However, in the light of Picasso's entire artistic career such a view, though maintained by critics with an axe to grind, like John Berger, has to be drastically revised. We can now see what Picasso was after, all along, in his insistence that it was the world he was interested in as much as art, and in his denunciation of Futurism, abstraction and the photomechanical production of art. As Leo Steinberg and others have shown, he went on till the very end exploring possible ways in which the multiple voices could be kept in play, and if he had dips in form or went down blind alleys then that is what engaging with the world through art is about. Rosalind Krauss is coy about the degree to which she believes that the charges of pastiche levelled at Picasso since that time are justified, and the degree to which she feels that he did indeed lose his way. But in her questioning of Berger and of his mentor Adorno, whose *Philosophy of Modern Music* she rightly sees as articulating most clearly the case against both Stravinsky (its immediate target) and Picasso, she is, as usual, both perceptive and profound. 'It is the historical logic of modernism', concludes her wonderful book on Picasso, that 'the newly liberated circulation of the token-sign always carries as its potential reverse an utterly devalued and empty currency. Pastiche is not necessarily the destiny of modernism, but it is its guilty conscience.'

Duchamp was the only other artist apart from Picasso to grasp this, so that actually to align him with Picabia and the new mechanisation of art is to do him an injustice. More clearly even than Picasso (he was the more cerebral artist), Duchamp understood what was at stake in the crisis of authority and tradition that had engulfed the arts in the last years of the nineteenth century, what it meant that 'the newly liberated circulation of the token-sign always carries as its potential reverse an utterly devalued and empty currency'. In an interview with Georges Charbonnier in 1961 he summed up his position with his customary wit:

> The word 'art', etymologically speaking, means to make, simply to make. Now what is making? Making something is choosing a tube of blue, a tube of red, putting some of it on the palette, and always choosing the quality of the blue, the quality of the red, and always choosing the place to put it on the canvas, it's always choosing. So in order to choose, you can use tubes of paint, you can use brushes, but you can also use a ready-made thing, made either mechanically or by the hand of another man, even, if you want, and appropriate it, since it's you who chose it. Choice is the main thing, even in normal painting.

In the old days the painter had been a craftsman, almost an alchemist. He alone knew how to mix the paints that led to his special effects, it was something that had been passed down to him from the master to whom he had been apprenticed, often his father, and he would in turn pass it on to his sons or apprentices. Once artists were able to buy paint ready-made in tubes open-air painting became possible, but something had also been lost (as with the coming of print for writers). The nineteenth century had seen a growing awareness of what was implied by choice, both in life and in art, and desperate attempts both by sensitive individuals and by ever more self-conscious artists to escape its arbitrariness. But 'Un coup de dés jamais n'abolira le hasard', and Duchamp draws the inescapable conclusion: since all art is choice and all choice is in the end arbitrary, a mere throw of the dice, why not face up to this fact, make one big choice right at the start and leave it at that? (Had not Kierkegaard's wise Judge in *Either/Or* made that the prescription for happiness?)

Of course, as we have seen in the case of Picasso, these things are always overdetermined. Though Duchamp made a big splash with his painting, *Nude Descending the Stairs*, the shock success of the Armory Show of 1913, he had never been much of a painter, so it is perhaps no surprise that in the years following that success he abandoned painting for ever and took up the idea of the readymade, first with his *Bicycle Wheel* (1913) and *Bottle Rack*

(1914), and then, in 1917, with his most famous work, the urinal he called *Fountain*. On the other hand it could be argued that he had never been very good at painting only *because* he had always been suspicious of it, had sensed from the start, what he was only to articulate much later, a deep suspicion of the whole enterprise of easel painting. Who can tell? (Who can tell why some sinners repent and others do not, some addicts manage to kick the habit and others do not?) In any case, as his most discerning critic, Thierry de Duve has shown in fascinating detail, the story of *Fountain* is a kind of parable, largely orchestrated by Duchamp, of the nature of art in our age. Readers of literature, eagerly snapping up the latest Goncourt or Booker Prize winner would do well to ponder its implications.

Duchamp submitted *Fountain* anonymously (he 'signed' it 'R. Mutt') to the hanging committee of the first exhibition of the American Society of Independent Artists, on whose jury he himself was. The society based itself on the Parisian society of the same name (the Salon des Indépendants) set up in 1884, to wrest control of the future of art from the Academy. In both cases the motto was the same: No jury, no prizes. In theory anyone could hang, for why should I, an independent artist, submit to the judgement of a jury of straight-laced traditionalists who wouldn't be able to discern good art if it was thrust into their faces? Duchamp had been invited onto the committee because of the triumph of his *Nude* at the Armory Show. His presence guaranteed the Independents' avant-garde credentials. Unfortunately neither life nor art is ever as simple as that. What the Independents of New York wanted was to be both liberal *and* avant-garde, to do what they wanted *and* have themselves proclaimed as important avant-garde artists. We have seen what such self-naming leads to in the case of Don Quixote and others. It was no different here. The Cervantes who drew the right conclusions from their efforts was, of course, Duchamp. By submitting not a new version of the *Nude*, but, anonymously, a signed urinal, he lit up, as with a flare, the contradictions of art today: for *Fountain* was, as everyone knows, rejected by the committee as obscene and 'not art'.

Actually, as de Duve shows, the story is a little more complicated than that, and Duchamp had to 'help' his readymade into the limelight. The offending object, anonymously submitted, would have simply disappeared had not Duchamp made sure it was photographed by the most famous photographer of the day, Alfred Stieglitz, and reproduced in a small satirical magazine, *The Blind Man*, whose first issue was devoted to the Independents' show. Thereafter *Fountain* literally disappeared, so that all we have is Stieglitz's photo, from which numerous models have of course been made and exhibited round the world, perhaps the most famous piece of modern art, and still as capable of dividing viewers as it ever was. Is it art? Is it art because of its intrinsic merits? Or because the institution says it is? And if the latter, does that mean that we have reached the end of art as it was known in the West since men began to draw in caves? It calls into question all competitions and all juries where art is concerned, and it reminds us of the dream of every artist (and all impresarios, whether publishers or galleries or agents) to be both unbeholden to any tradition and yet proclaimed King of the New.

Had Beethoven had Mozart's lyric gifts, Stravinsky says somewhere in his conversations with Robert Craft, he would never have developed his rhythmic capacities to the degree that he did. Duchamp was always more interested in conceptions than in the possibilities of drawing or working in three dimensions. When he took a bottle-rack or a urinal and relabelled them and exhibited them, he made all those who saw what he had done think again and think hard about what constitutes a work of art, what the function of art is in our society, what it is that gives us pleasure, what our relation is to the objects we use in everyday life, etc., etc. When Picasso took a toy car and made of it the head of a monkey he saw in what he had made something touching and funny and added a baby monkey clinging to the mother's belly, calling the whole thing *Mother and Child*. The wit is as sharp as Duchamp's, but there is more: his welded sculpture tells us something about monkeys, about ourselves, and about mothers and their children. It's absurd to ask which is better, Duchamp or Picasso. Both, in a sense, fulfil the Bakhtinian principle of releasing the multiple voices which would not have been given a hearing had something not been made (or nudged into being) by an artist.

Both Picasso and Duchamp grasped what was at issue, and both have their 'descendants'. Those of Duchamp have of course grabbed more of the headlines, though it is difficult not to feel that, in their case, the Master has made them redundant. Duchamp himself, supreme ironist that he was, was extremely reticent in what he chose to say and extremely choosy about the art he subsequently chose to make, thereby, in Kierkegaard's terms, retaining our trust in him as a 'real' artist. His descendants and disciples, lacking the clarity of his insight into what is really at issue, have been less parsimonious. Picasso's descendants have had, so to speak, a larger field to play in. One of the chief among them is of course Bacon. We have already examined his contrast between 'illustration' and the sort of art he himself was trying to make, but he was equally forthright about abstraction. Talking to David Sylvester about the great Rembrandt self-portrait in Aix-en-Provence (*figure 5*), he points out that 'if you analyze it, you will see that there are hardly any sockets to the eyes, that it is almost completely anti-illustrational'. And he adds:

> I think that the mystery of fact is conveyed by an image being made out of non-rational marks. And you can't will this non-rationality of a mark. That is the reason that accident always has to enter into this activity, because the moment you know what to do, you're making just another form of illustration. But what can happen sometimes, as it happened in this Rembrandt self-portrait, is that there is a coagulation of non-representational marks which have led to making up this very great image. Well, of course, only part of this is accidental. Behind all that is Rembrandt's profound sensibility which was able to hold onto one irrational mark rather than onto another.

Bacon is trying to say something very difficult, and very close to himself as a painter, and it is a tribute to David Sylvester that he takes the trouble. What differentiates a painter like him (and Picasso) from someone like Duchamp, this passage suggests, is that while he is just as aware of the chance nature of the marks he is making, he also has a sense that he can, because of who he is, because of what he has learned in the course of his life, make a more than merely arbitrary choice about which marks to reinforce, which to ignore, and here he is claiming Rembrandt as a precursor. But he immediately notes that abstract expressionists too have claimed Rembrandt as a precursor, and he goes on to

figure 5 Rembrandt van Rijn, *Self-Portrait, c.* 1659.

differentiate himself from them. With Rembrandt, he says, the marks have been done in

> an attempt to record a fact and to me therefore must be much more exciting and much more profound. One of the reasons why I don't like abstract painting, or why it doesn't interest me, is that I think painting is a duality, and that abstract painting is an entirely aesthetic thing. It always remains on one level. It is only really interested in the beauty of its patterns or its shapes. We know that most people, especially artists, have large areas of undisciplined emotion, and I think that abstract artists believe that in these marks they're making they are catching all these sorts of emotions. But I think that, caught in that way, they are too weak to convey anything . . . You see, I believe that art is recording; I think it's reporting. And I think that in abstract art, as there's no report, there's nothing other than the aesthetic of the painter and his few sensations. There's never any tension in it.

Rembrandt (and Bacon), he is saying, are taken out of themselves by the object before them, which moves them so deeply that they want to make it live again through their own efforts. So they owe a double allegiance: to the object out there in the world, and to the artwork. Abstract painters, he suggests, only have allegiance to the artwork, and to themselves. Hence the work will lack what he feels to be a vital ingredient. Sylvester, however, is puzzled: 'If abstract paintings are no more than pattern-making, how do you explain the fact that there are people like myself who have the same sort of visceral response to them at times as they have to figurative work?' Bacon will have no truck with this. 'Fashion', he replies imperiously. But lest we be tempted to dismiss this as too glib, let us remember Joseph Koerner's comment on Friedrich and the claims that have been made for him as the precursor of abstract expressionism.

The problem of abstraction and the problem of how to deal with Duchampian scepticism would seem to be issues confined to the visual arts, but that is not the case. Just as Krauss could use Adorno's (misguided) critique of Stravinsky to make a point about Picasso, so we should be able to move from problems which first surfaced in the realm of painting to music and literature. The divide between Duchamp and Picasso is clearly evident in the divide between John Cage and his followers on the one hand, and composers such as Stockhausen, Boulez, Nono, Ligeti and Kurtág, on the other. These composers, who all came of age in the years immediately following the end of the Second World War, believed that the war and the devastation it had brought had given them a chance to start again, in a sense, ignoring for the most part the traditions of classical and Romantic music. But whereas Cage, the American, opted for a version of Duchampian scepticism, the Europeans found their inspiration in medieval and Renaissance music and the musics of the far East and central Africa. In place of Cage's Buddhist-inspired irony there was a new idealism, a new sense of being able to go forward, inspired by the work of their early Modernist predecessors, Schoenberg, Webern, Stravinsky and Varèse. In time, of course, some of them, like Berio and Kurtág, even found a place in their work for Schubert and Mahler. Where Cage and his followers drew the conclusion that *all* traditions were dead, they began to forge new, more inclusive traditions, though always aware that their relation to them could never be that which had obtained in the time of Bach or Haydn.

But what of literature? As it happens there is a nice example to hand of how the Picasso moment of 1912 is destined to be played out again and again whenever Modernism is in question. In the 1950s a young French agronomist who had briefly been a prisoner of war in Germany and then worked on banana plantations in Africa, began to try his hand at the writing of fiction, first with short stories and then with a mysterious novel based on *Oedipus Rex* in which the detective detailed to investigate a murder finds that the murder has not (yet) taken place, and ends up committing it himself. Clearly what interested the young Robbe-Grillet in the Greek tragedy was its inexorable quality, the fact that there is nothing arbitrary in the plotting, that all unfolds with the relentlessness of a machine. In his subsequent novels, *Le Voyeur*, *La Jalousie* and *Dans Le Labyrinthe*, he found his voice and produced a series of masterpieces. As his most acute critic, Maurice Blanchot, immediately discerned, the cold, precise descriptive style Robbe-Grillet perfected had nothing to do with hyper-realism but rather was the means of articulating a nightmare vision in which the light is always at maximum brightness but its source remains mysteriously hidden, in which something has possibly taken place which the narrative not only cannot articulate but is at pains to conceal even from itself. In *Le Voyeur* it is the murder of a child; in *La Jalousie* it is an act of marital betrayal. These novels are like no others, but they do conform to the Mallarméan injunctions: they proceed by means of hypothesis and by short cuts, and the anecdote is eschewed. Because the obsessive consciousness is at the heart of each, the author is released from the need to tell a story, to move on from event to event, with the sense that this would bring with it of the thinness and insubstantiality of what is being depicted, as well as of its arbitrary nature. Instead, as in Pinget, we have the impression of a field being explored; when it has been thoroughly tilled the book ends, leaving us with a powerful sense of having undergone an intense if inarticulate experience.

The feeling of being in a labyrinth from which it is impossible to escape, already strong in Robbe-Grillet's first novel, *Les Gommes*, is most clearly evident in his fourth, *Dans le Labyrinthe*. But in this story, of a soldier seeking to deliver a parcel the contents of which he does not know in a town which is both familiar and unfamiliar, the compulsive centre from which the previous two novels had radiated is less intense – there is no crime or outrage to explain why it is the soldier wanders in his labyrinth. The story, with its rhythms of returning again and again to the same spot, hovers between the terrifying and the pleasurable, perhaps the kind of pleasure Hans Castorp in *The Magic Mountain* felt he would experience if he lay down in the snow and allowed himself to doze off. The rhythms of the sentences and of the movements of the soldier, for ever striving forward but getting nowhere, lull us into a kind of will-less concentration, such as those who meditate tell us they experience. It is Robbe-Grillet's most beautiful book, held in a kind of gentle tension, like some of Wallace Stevens's greatest poems, between meaning and the abandonment of meaning, mysterious, like them, and, like them, precise in every word.

But after that novel something seems to have happened to Robbe-Grillet's work. It is as if he had suddenly discovered that the free circulation of the sign, to use Rosalind Krauss's terminology, had made it possible for him to do anything he wished, and henceforth he does just that – but at the cost of leaving us indifferent to what he is doing, leaving us, in effect, just as Bacon described himself left by abstract art, bored by the lack of tension. We were certainly not indifferent to what was unfolding in *Le Voyeur* and *La Jalousie*, even if we were unclear as to just *what* was unfolding. We wanted to know the outcome even as we came to realise that we never would. From his fifth novel on, we can admire Robbe-Grillet's pellucid style but we cease to have any interest in his books. Unfortunately too, for Robbe-Grillet as for his fellow-novelist Claude Simon, this was just the moment when the brilliant critic Jean Ricardou began to publish his spirited defence of the *nouveau roman* – but a defence that was so powerful, so fool-proof precisely because it started from the premise that the free circulation of the sign meant that art had finally, thankfully, cut itself off from the world and had only itself to worry about. In a famous debate Robbe-Grillet claimed that he began from a word and let it carry him where it would, while Nathalie Sarraute, the 'mother' of the *nouveau roman*, insisted that one began with a darkness which one felt the need to penetrate. Robbe-Grillet would have none of this: Kandinsky and the Surrealists, Picabia and Pop Art had, in effect, for him, replaced Picasso. Only Pinget and Duras, the least intellectual of the group, continued to develop, producing works that were at times flawed, at times embarrassingly bad, but also at times masterpieces of the order of *Passacaille* or *L'Amante anglaise*. There is no clearer indication that in the field of literature as well as in the fine arts, Picasso's instinctive aversion to both abstraction and the mass-produced was the result of his correct intuition as to where lay the health of art and the true destiny of Modernism.

11

A Clown, Perhaps, But An Aspiring Clown

I grow old . . . I grow old . . .
I shall wear the bottoms of my trousers rolled.

Shall I part my hair behind? Do I dare to eat a peach?
I shall wear white flannel trousers, and walk upon the beach.
I have heard the mermaids singing, each to each.

I do not think that they will sing to me.

I have seen them riding seaward on the waves
Combing the white hair of the waves blown back
When the wind blows the water white and black.

We have lingered by the chambers of the sea
By sea-girls wreathed with seaweed red and brown
Till human voices wake us, and we drown.

At first sight the form and title of the poem – 'The Love Song of J. Alfred Prufrock' – suggest that it is, like one of Browning's monologues, an exercise in characterisation. But this soon turns out to be an error. Eliot's poem too insistently breaks down the boundaries between the main character, the writer and the reader: Prufrock is not a figure from the past but from the present, not someone 'out there' but someone uncomfortably 'in here', not someone with a story to tell but only someone who seems to feel the need to speak. It's true that the speaker is given a name and a comic name at that, but this is a lure, an attempt by the poet to isolate his anxieties by dramatising them, much as Hamlet 'puts an antic disposition on'. In fact, we soon realise, the poem is really a kind of ode, like Wordsworth's Immortality Ode or Keats's 'Ode to Melancholy', a poem in which the first person speaks for all of us and speaks in order not to instruct but to understand. And just as we have to take the pronouncements of Wordsworth and Keats seriously, so here, when Eliot/Prufrock says: 'I have heard the mermaids singing each to each./ I do not think that they will sing to me', we must take him as seriously as we would take the pronouncements of any poet. Were he prepared to roll up the bottoms of his trousers and walk upon the beach without self-consciousness all would perhaps be well. He would be a novelist, perhaps, or a minor poet, commenting on the seascape. Were the mermaids to sing to him as the Muses sang to Homer all would be well. He would write down their words and be the spokesman of the community. But no, he has heard the mermaids singing and so can never again return to his old life; but because they weren't singing to him but only to each other, he is in the unenviable position of having to live with the sense that what would give meaning to his life is there, but just out of earshot. 'There is salvation', as Kafka once said, 'but not for us.'

In such a situation the very notion of a craft of poetry becomes a mockery. The two lines, 'I shall wear white flannel trousers, and walk upon the beach', and 'I have heard the mermaids singing each to each' form a perfect rhyming couplet, but the rhyme remains empty because 'each to each' turns in on itself and remains, semantically, in a different universe from that of the poet walking on the beach. Hence what follows is a line that cannot have a rhyme because it is a description of solitude and loss: 'I do not think that they will sing to me.'

Of course the world of so-called culture (what Pound ironically Americanised as *Kulchur*) goes on its way, as it always does, blithely unaware that anything is amiss: 'In the room the women come and go/ Talking of Michelangelo.' Pope too used the rhyming couplet to signal the disjunction rather than the conjunction between the ideal world and the social world, but in Eliot the disjunction goes deeper because there is no sense that a change in the attitudes of society would set things right, only the bleak acknowledgement that things are not right. After such knowledge, how is lyric poetry any longer possible? (A question that Eliot is asking not only long before Adorno postulated it in the aftermath of Auschwitz, but even before the First World War, for 'Prufrock' was written in 1911.)

Yet the final lines do seem to salvage something from the wreck: the speaker will never be able to hear what the mermaids are saying, but, like Wallace Stevens in his great poems of the sea, he manages to convey something of its voice in his image of the ever oncoming and outgoing waves:

> I have seen them riding seaward on the waves
> Combing the white hair of the waves blown back
> When the wind blows the water white and black.

The final triplet, however, reminds us that our sense of what the mermaids are and what they may be saying is a precarious one, which will last only as long as we are reading (and the poet is writing) the poem: when we look up from it, in the end, 'human voices wake us, and we drown'. We are left with the disintegrating vision and with the insistent and meaningless rhyme of 'red and brown'/ 'and we drown'.

Wallace Stevens was Eliot's older contemporary, but where Eliot was already famous by 1922 as the author of *The Waste Land* and *The Sacred Wood*, Stevens had not yet published his first volume, *Harmonium*, and even after the appearance of that wonderful collection in 1923, was not recognised as a major poet till he was in his fifties. With hindsight, though, we can see that the longest poem in *Harmonium*, 'The Comedian as the Letter C', is *his* version of 'Prufrock', his version of the portrait of the artist as a young man in our modern world. This time, though, it is a very American world.

Stevens here, as in so many of his poems, instinctively adopts what Kierkegaard called 'the dialectic principle': first you posit this, then you posit its opposite, then you see what happens. Part I, 'The World Without Imagination', tells how Crispin, on solid ground, trying to anchor his being in himself, finds himself overwhelmed by the sea:

> Sed quaeritur: is this same wig
> Of things, this nincompated pedagogue,
> Preceptor to the sea? Crispin at sea
> Created, in his day, a touch of doubt.
> An eye most apt in gelatines and jupes

> Berries of villages, a barber's eye,
> An eye of land, of simple salad-beds,
> Of honest quilts, the eye of Crispin, hung
> On porpoises, instead of apricots,
> And on silentious porpoises, whose snouts
> Dibbled in waves that were mustachios,
> Inscrutable hair in an inscrutable world.

This, we feel, is crazy. It's closer to Lewis Carroll and Edward Lear than it is to serious poetry. But, as Elizabeth Sewell showed many years ago, Carroll and Lear have just as much right to be incorporated into the story of nineteenth- and twentieth-century poetry as Mallarmé and Rimbaud. Indeed, they are the playful reverse image of those two poets, and what we have in Stevens, as he struggles to understand the nature of his gift and his vocation, is the coming together of the two traditions. The sign, the word, is always threatening to take off into sound, 'circulating freely', as Krauss puts it, and leaving the signified, the semantic content of the word, behind. That is both the problem and the challenge for Stevens; for us the secret is to keep moving.

We are immediately rewarded. 'Crispin was washed away by magnitude', we read in the next stanza. He is dissolved in the sea,

> nothing left of him,
> Except in faint, memorial gesturings,
> That were like arms and shoulders in the waves,
> Here, something in the rise and fall of wind
> That seemed hallucinating horn, and here,
> A sunken voice, both of remembering
> And of forgetfulness, in alternate strain.
> Just so an ancient Crispin was dissolved
> The valet in the tempest was annulled.

But just as Friedrich's *Rückenfigur* stands between us and the annihilated world of mist and sea, so now Crispin rises again as a comic *Rückenfigur*, protecting us from dissolution. In Part III, 'Approaching Carolina', we find him trying to find a balance between annihilation by the sea and the need to settle down and live. It would be easy to forget the sea, to lead a useful life, even to write poems, for the moonlight fills his mind with stories and ideas. Yet Crispin is wary:

> How many poems he denied himself
> In his observant progress, lesser things
> Than the relentless contact he desired.

Moonlight, he senses, is an evasion, 'mere poetry', when what he longs for, like Francis Bacon, is the 'relentless contact' with reality. Such contact, however, he knows, would bring annihilation with it. But what if he were to forget the annihilating sea and celebrate the ordinary?

> A river bore
> The vessel inward. Tilting up his nose,
> He inhaled the rancid rosin, burly smells
> Of dampened lumber, emanations blown
> From warehouse doors, the gustiness of ropes,
> Decays of sacks, and all the arrant stinks
> That helped him round his rude aesthetic out.

This has always been the dream of American writing and it is at the heart of Stevens's friend and contemporary, William Carlos Williams, and there again in Saul Bellow's most American book, *The Adventures of Augie March*: 'I am an American, Chicago born – Chicago, that somber city – and go at things as I have taught myself, free-style, and will make the record in my own way: first to knock, first admitted; sometimes an innocent knock, sometimes a not so innocent.' But anchoring the twentieth-century American drunken boat in 'rancid rosin, burly smells' and all the rest turns out, for Crispin, to be as much of a dream as everything else. In Part IV, 'The Idea of a Colony', we see him setting up his colony, determined to 'make new intelligence prevail', yet at the end he has to confess that

> He could not be content with counterfeit,
> With masquerade of thought, with hapless words
> That must belie the racking masquerade,

With fictive flourishes that preordained
His passion's permit, hang of coat, degree
Of buttons, measure of his salt. Such trash
Might help the blind, not him, serenely sly.
It irked beyond his patience.

Perhaps, then, since he can neither reach the 'essential prose' nor
do without it, what he has to do is what Donne long ago recommended: 'He who would truth find/ About must and about must
go.' Sly Crispin accepts that his only role may be that of clown: 'A
clown, perhaps, but an aspiring clown.' In keeping with this the last
two sections are entitled 'A Nice Shady Home' and 'And Daughters
with Curls'. He 'who once planned/ Loquacious columns by the
ructive sea' is now content to build himself a cabin inland, in the
American way, and to father four daughters. Is this a sell-out? He
concludes, with one of those 'if' sentences that gives even as it takes
away:

Or if the music sticks, if the anecdote
Is false, if Crispin is a profitless
Philosopher, beginning with green brag
Concluding fadedly, if as a man
Prone to distemper he abates in taste,
Fickle and fumbling, variable, obscure,
Glozing his life with after-shining flicks . . .
Making gulped portions from obstreperous drops,
And so distorting, proving what he proves
Is nothing, what can all this matter since
The relation comes, benignly, to its end?

The 'relation' is of course both the telling and the fact that
Crispin is not alone in the world, even if he sometimes feels that
way. And so, after a gap to let the question mark do its work, the
last line of the poem compresses all its themes together, playing
with the meaning of 'clipped': trimmed, as of a hedge, and, in its
old meaning, found in Shakespeare, embraced: 'So may the relation of each man be clipped.'

What Stevens learned in 'The Comedian as the Letter C' is that,
like Picasso, it was the angel of reality he was after, but that to get

at him you had to work dialectically and by indirection. It was a lesson that would stand him in good stead in the years to come.

Over in Europe at the close of that same crucial decade, the second of the century, Franz Kafka brought out one of the few books he would publish in his lifetime, a collection of fourteen stories, mainly written during the war, entitled *A Country Doctor*. As always, Kafka was meticulous about the order and the arrangement. The story he chose to open the collection is no more than a page long, but it is one of his greatest. It is called 'The New Advocate', and is, in a sense, his 'Prufrock', his 'Comedian as the Letter C'. 'We have a new advocate, Dr. Bucephalus', it begins. 'There is little in his appearance to remind you that he was once Alexander of Macedon's warhorse. Of course, if you know his story, you are aware of something.' But even the usher at the law courts, who presumably does not know his story, though he is, it is true, 'a man with the professional eye of one who regularly places small bets at racecourses', finds himself 'running an admiring eye over the advocate as he mounted the marble steps with a high action that made them ring beneath his feet'.

However, this high-stepping urge is now kept well under control, for 'nowadays . . . there is no Alexander the Great'. Of course, even in Alexander's day, 'the gates of India were beyond reach, yet the King's sword pointed the way to them'. Today, however, no-one even points the way – for in which direction would they point? Many, it is true, still carry swords, 'but only to brandish them, and the eye that tries to follow them is confused'. So 'perhaps it is really best to do as Bucephalus has done, and absorb oneself in law books. In the quiet lamplight, his flanks unhampered by the thighs of a rider, free and far from the clamour of battle, he reads and turns the pages of our ancient tomes.'

A loss has been incurred, yet the last little paragraph is neither pathetic nor anguished, merely resigned: 'Perhaps it is really best to do as Bucephalus has done.' Bucephalus, like Prufrock, like Crispin, can no longer summon up the energy to fly in the face of reality, like Don Quixote. His flanks are at least unhampered by the thighs of any rider – yet we recall the high action of his legs as he strides up the staircase of the law-courts and feel the waste: a rider pressing into those flanks would at least have given him a goal, a sense of direction. Instead, he consoles himself by poring over ancient law books, though whether he does this out of a sense of duty, or desire, or merely to pass the time, the story does not say.

The fourth of my sad clowns comes in the form not of words but of images – and a very unusual image it is. Here is what its creator had to say about it many years later:

> From Munich on, I had the idea of the Large Glass. I was finished with cubism ... The whole trend of painting was something I didn't care to continue ... There was no essential satisfaction for me in painting ever. And then of course I just wanted to react against what the others were doing, Matisse and all the rest, all that work of the hand. In French there is an old expression, *la patte*, meaning the artist's touch, his personal style, his 'paw'. I wanted to get away from *la patte* and from all that retinal painting.

Duchamp was to describe the work that he now (1914–21) embarked on as 'a delay in glass', but the title he gave it was: *La Mariée mise à nu par ses célibataires, même* ('The Bride Laid Bare By Her Bachelors, Even'), an odd title couched in odd grammar, but not at all untypical of Duchamp and actually a good deal more comprehensible than some. On two large rectangular glass panels, one below the other, each encased in a metal frame, the whole free-standing, a number of elements are painted: in the top panel is the Bride herself, a wavy cloud lacking all clear outline, with three square holes in the middle, and, hanging from the left-hand side, something like a pulled-out wall socket, giving the whole a vaguely insect-like quality; in the lower panel there is a precisely painted larger-than-life chocolate-grinder (a faithful copy of a machine found by Duchamp in his native Rouen), a group of what could be stylised clothes-pegs, a kind of pulley contraption, and a number of circular diagrams such as one finds in opticians' offices, above which an eyehole has been cut into the glass.

It may help to recall *Either/Or*, the first part of which is spoken/written by a young man, a bachelor, only too aware of his historical condition and the impossibility of meaningful choice in today's world, and the second by a maturer man, a Judge, happily married, who argues that once the young man has made the leap into marriage, the transition from bachelor to husband, all his troubles will be solved. The problem is that the young man feels he has no grounds for choosing one woman rather than another, and, moreover, he has the sneaking suspicion that any choice would be a disaster, robbing him of life's most precious quality, freedom. Yet at the same time he acknowledges – and he is quite genuine here – that the Judge may well be right and that it is his fault that he cannot make the leap into marriage. The book, as the title implies, sets the two up against each other but refuses to occupy a position above both, from which it might be possible to adjudicate between them. Duchamp's *Large Glass* is his *Either/Or*. It is also his 'Prufrock', his ironical self-portrait as an artist in troubled times. It is both his farewell to painting and his examination, tongue in cheek as always, of why painting has reached the pass it has. It is the early twentieth-century version of Durer's *Melencolia I*.

The Bachelors below may grind out their chocolate, but they are clearly powerless to reach the Bride, just as the artist can no longer approach his sacred subject. The erotic subtext is clear and again typical of Duchamp, as it is of Sterne: the futile, mechanical, masturbation of the Bachelors will never lead to any congruence with the Bride, far less to any offspring. But this is perhaps too simple. After all, there is not one bridegroom or even fiancé, but a group of Bachelors – who perhaps are doomed to remain bachelors because what they long for cannot be attained. Thierry de Duve suggests that the idea of stripping the Bride bare relates to Duchamp's sense of the new moves towards abstraction, which painters like Kandinsky, Malevich and Mondrian were convinced would lay bare the essence of art (once figuration, the world, had been stripped away). He also suggests that the chocolate-grinder relates to the old notion, already touched on above, that once painters used to grind out their own colours, but now buy them ready-made. The chocolate grinder is thus both an emblem of industrialisation, that industrialisation which has rendered painting meaningless, and an emblem of a kind of pre-industrialisation (since now we more often buy our chocolate already ground), for which we are all, and artists in particular, so nostalgic.

But why 'A delay in glass'? Partly of course because of the delay, which will stretch to infinity, between the desires of the Bachelors and the embrace of the Bride. But also because the work is so made that we cannot take it in at one go as we can all paintings, however complex, and however often we need to return to them to flesh out that initial 'retinal' impression. Because it is painted on glass and because the object is free-standing, as we look we see not only what is *on* the glass but also, *through* the glass, the room beyond and the other visitors looking at the art in this room. The peep-hole on the right-hand side of the lower panel is a further source of perplexity, for it implies an opaque surface, a closed door such as Duchamp will create for his last work, *Etant Donnés* ('Being Given'), a wooden surface breached by a single tiny circular hole to which the eye can be put. Here, however, looking through the peep-hole, perhaps imagining that it will reveal some further, as yet unseen, vision, we see only what we could already see through the glass.

The work is extremely beautiful and meticulously made, Duchamp spending eight years transferring its elements – the Bride above and the 'Bachelor Machine' below – from sketches and preliminary works onto the two glass panels. *The Large Glass*, as it has come to be known, is also accompanied by boxes of detailed notes on physics, alchemy, metaphysics and much else, which – Duchamp being Duchamp – it is difficult to know whether to take seriously or as a spoof. They have of course, like the novels of Thomas Bernhard, to be taken both ways.

Today the original stands in the Philadelphia Museum of Fine Art, but there is a copy by Richard Hamilton in Tate Modern in London. Yet, unlike *Fountain*, which both does not exist anywhere and yet can exist in multiple sets, the Philadelphia Glass is unique, and the story of why it is unique is wonderfully Duchampian. Duchamp finished *The Large Glass* in 1921, in time for it to be exhibited at a show in New York. In transit from Philadelphia to New York, however, the two glass panels, which had been laid one on top of the other but not well enough insulated, ground against each other and, when the work was removed from its packaging on arrival, both panels were found to be shattered. Duchamp was immediately summoned to see if he could repair the damage, but when he looked at it he let out a whoop of joy, for the work now had a giant rainbow of cracks on the top panel mirrored by a similar pattern on the lower one. And one can see why he was so delighted. For years he had been trying to bring chance into his work, but chance brought in by the artist is never exactly chance. Now chance had led to an unexpected copulation in the back of a van and the result was a beautiful pattern which bound the top panel to the lower, while, amazingly, leaving all the main elements of the object perfectly visible and the whole still capable of standing up. He could not have asked for more from the gods.

Today far more visitors see Richard Hamilton's copy (made for the great English Duchamp exhibition of 1966, since the *Large Glass* could never be moved again) than ever see the original in Philadelphia. They think they are seeing it all, but of course they are not. The work they see is still very beautiful – but it is, somehow, dead. In Philadelphia, with its rainbow shatterings, it lives.

12

I Would Prefer Not To

When Bartleby is asked by his employer to do something, it will be remembered, he takes to answering: 'I would prefer not to.' In an interview with his dealer, Daniel-Henri Kahnweiler, Picasso recalled: 'I well remember what I told [Braque and Gris] in the cubist room at the Indépendants, where there were some Gleizes and Metzingers: "I thought we'd enjoy ourselves a bit, but it's getting bloody boring again." ' 'The whole scaffolding of art bores me and gives me a headache', remarks Thomas Mann's composer-hero, Adrian Leverkühn. And Beckett: 'I speak of an art . . . weary of puny exploits, weary of pretending to be able, of being able, of doing a little better the same old thing, of going a little further along a dreary road.' On a lighter note Salinger's Holden Caulfield begins his narrative:

> If you really want to hear about it, the first thing you'll probably want to know is where I was born and what my lousy childhood was like and how my parents were occupied and all before they had me, and all that David Copperfield kind of crap, but I don't feel like going into it, if you want to know the truth. In the first place, that stuff bores me.

In all these cases doing something other people seem to have no difficulty in doing becomes an intolerable imposition, not because it is fiendishly difficult but because it is so boring. And what makes a thing boring? That it is meaningless, and that therefore spending time on it feels as though it were robbing one of a portion of one's life. None of the other toilers in Wall Street appears to feel this, but Bartleby does. Picasso does. Leverkühn does. Beckett does. Holden Caulfield does. In the case of Picasso that is a sign that he must move on, find something less boring, more meaningful, to do, but the others don't seem to have that option. For them it seems to be a question of either boring themselves to death or giving up altogether. Kafka's Hunger Artist is their patron saint. He has lain dying of hunger in the straw of his circus cage for days before he is noticed.

> They poked into the straw with sticks and found him in it. 'Are you still fasting?' asked the overseer, 'when on earth do you mean to stop?' 'Forgive me, everybody', whispered the hunger artist; only the overseer, who had his ear to the bars, understood him. 'Of course', said the overseer, and tapped his forehead with a finger to let the attendants know what state the man was in, 'we forgive you.' 'I always wanted you to admire my fasting', said the hunger artist. 'We do admire it', said the overseer, affably. 'But you shouldn't admire it', said the hunger artist. 'Well then we don't admire it', said the overseer, 'but why shouldn't we admire it?' 'Because I have to fast, I can't help it', said the hunger artist. 'What a fellow you are', said the overseer, 'and why can't you help it?' 'Because', said the hunger artist, lifting his head a little and speaking with his lips pursed, as if for a kiss, right into the overseer's ear, so that no syllable might be lost, 'because I couldn't find the food I liked. If I had found it, believe me, I should have made no fuss and stuffed myself like you or anyone else.' These were his last words, but in his dimming eyes remained the firm though no longer proud persuasion that he was still continuing to fast.

The young Kafka dreamed of becoming a writer in order to escape the meaninglessness of the life he saw around him, in the first instance the life of his parents. Like all artists, he dreamed also, no doubt, of fame and glory. As he watched that fame and glory settle effortlessly on the shoulders of his friends Franz Werfel and Max Brod, while his own writing passed, for the most part, into obscurity, he struggled to understand what was happening. He knew their work was meretricious, sentimental, littered with cliché – yet was his own any better? Could the public be that wrong? Was it not rather his own work, obscure, crabbed, incomprehensible sometimes even to himself, that was without merit? After all, Werfel and Brod at least gave pleasure to thousands while his writing hardly even gave pleasure to himself. All he could say, at the end of his life, when 'The Hunger Artist' was written, was that he had had no option. His very body shied away from following the path of Werfel and Brod. Had his body accepted it he would have gone willingly down that path, but it didn't. It couldn't process food like that and so he couldn't eat it, and if the alternative was starvation, so be it. He mostly took no pride in this, had no wish to boast that *they* were *passé*, old hat, while *his* was the way of the future, as would one day be acknowledged. All he knew was that he could not do it. He who had not been able to find nourishment in a job, in a prospective marriage, who had imagined that writing would provide it, had come to see at last that writing could not help him either. More than that, as his anguished 1922 letter to Brod, from which I quoted at the start, suggests, he felt, like the young Wordsworth in the nut wood, that by writing he was desecrating, polluting, God's earth. All he had been was a burden and a disappointment to his family and friends and the sooner he was dead the better.

> 'Well, clear this out now!' said the overseer, and they buried the hunger artist, straw and all. Into the cage they put a young panther. Even the most insensitive felt it refreshing to see this wild creature leaping around the cage that had so long been dreary . . . His noble body, furnished almost to bursting point with all that it needed, seemed to carry freedom around with it too; somewhere in his jaws it seemed to lurk; and the joy of life streamed with such ardent passion from his throat that for the onlookers it was not easy to stand the shock of it.

Clearly what we might call the threshold of boredom is different for different people. For Duchamp the very thought of painting became a horror. And when Stieglitz asked him in 1922 for his views on photography, no doubt expecting support from his new ally, Duchamp replied, in very Beckettian style: 'Dear Stieglitz, Even a few words I don't feel like writing. You know exactly how I feel about photography. I would like to see it make people despise painting until something else will make photography unbearable.

There we are. Affectueusement, Marcel Duchamp.' For Jarry, Ionesco and Beckett, the idea of having people on a stage pretend to be 'characters' embroiled in a 'plot' is something they cannot countenance. They have to make it clear from the start that what they are doing is completely ridiculous, preposterous in fact, and they find different ways of doing so and then of filling up the length of time an audience expects to sit in a theatre. Jarry turns to Grand Guignol for his inspiration and starts his play with the one word nobody had ever thought to utter on stage: 'Merde!' (Ubu actually says 'merdre', which adds an element of wit to the scatological humour); Ionesco discovers that he can use a manual for learning English to determine the nature of the characters and what they say to each other; Beckett that he can fill the time by having two characterless characters talk about how they are filling in the time. Pinter and Bernhard, on the other hand, seem able to put on stage characters who are at least recognisable, even if extreme, and to abide by the conventions of realism even if they strain them at every turn. In fact seeing how far these artistic conventions (which mesh of course with the conventions by which bourgeois society lives) can be strained, becomes part of what drives their dramaturgy. In fiction Beckett again, from *Molloy* onwards, finds himself compelled to do away with most of the trappings of the novel, while Nabokov seems able and happy to work within them. In all these cases the borders of what they 'prefer not to' do are slightly different, and in every instance, one feels, it is not the mind that decides, but – one almost wants to say – the body.

Is the threshold even constant for the lifetime of an artist? One can see a poet like Eliot or a playwright like Stoppard moving from a fairly radical to a relatively moderate approach and style as they grow older – and are we sure that what we are witnessing is a decline? What is certain is the truth of Barthes' remark that 'to be modern is to know that which is not possible any more'. And this suggests that Modernism is, historically, deeply intertwined with the emergence of a critical conscience. This is as true of Rabelais and Cervantes in the Renaissance as it is of Wordsworth, Mallarmé and Eliot. And is the Preface to the *Lyrical Ballads* not the first avant-garde manifesto in Western cultural history? 'They who have been accustomed to the gaudiness and inane phraseology of many modern writers', writes Wordsworth, 'if they persist in reading this book to its conclusion, will, no doubt, frequently have to struggle with feelings of strangeness and awkwardness: they will look round for poetry, and will be induced to inquire by what species of courtesy these attempts can be permitted to assume that title.' Eliot could have said the same thing about *his* first volume of poetry, and we have seen Evelyn Waugh's response to Picasso: 'Very interesting, no doubt, but not art.'

I recently shared a platform with an eminent English novelist with a passion for art, who amused the audience by telling them that Mondrian felt he could not make any diagonal lines. 'I feel there are no limits', she said. 'Why should we not make diagonal lines if we want to?' This sounds like an admirable sentiment, a robust assertion of artistic independence. But if we look into the case of Mondrian, his denial is clearly not a kowtowing to the unspoken rules of society, but comes from some deep impulse within the artist himself. Mondrian's search was, from the start, not for beauty but for truth. He gravitated towards the grid because the grid implies that pictures have no beginnings and no ends, and no heroic or bucolic drama either, unless it is a factitious one introduced by the artist. He wanted to escape from such arbitrariness and at the same time to acknowledge the human and physical dimension of painting. As one of his most perceptive critics, Yve-Alain Bois, has remarked: 'The essential argument in Mondrian's famous critique of Theo van Doesberg's use of oblique lines [is that it] presupposes, according to Mondrian, an eye liberated from the human body: neoplasticism is "the true and pure manifestation of cosmic equilibrium from which, as human beings, we cannot separate ourselves".' One can disagree with the premise, as one can disagree with this or that pronouncement of Beckett or Bernhard, but what one cannot do is dismiss what they are doing, or rather what they refuse to do, as merely cranky, like only eating nuts.

Francis Bacon explained to David Sylvester that what he was trying to do was to get away from the anecdote and make his paintings more immediate.

> How many poems he denied himself
> In his observant progress, lesser things
> Than the relentless contact he desired

we remember Wallace Stevens's Comedian saying. Perhaps in the end it is the search for this 'relentless contact' that explains what makes all these artists feel that there are things they cannot do, things that bore them beyond endurance – from Rabelais to Picasso and from Cervantes to Schoenberg. What they want is to make something that will be as alive as the world they inhabit, something that, in Barthes' words, possesses 'the trembling of existence (*le tremblement de l'existence*)'; they are made sick by the thought that all the tradition seems to offer them is, instead, 'a world which is constructed, elaborated, detached', a world in which everything has its place, in which everything, even the most terrible, has 'a peaceful look, an air of respectful decency, which comes of their being held beneath a gaze fixed at infinity,' as Merleau-Ponty put it. Sometimes they feel that the way to escape this, to experience that relentless contact, is through a torrent of words and invective, as in Beckett or Bernhard. Sometimes they try to do it by a sly subversion of what is expected, as when Eliot fills the empty form of the quatrain, so popular with the Georgians, with vocabulary far from Georgian, and in doing so brings the nonsense verse of Lear and Carroll back into the mainstream of poetry:

> The broad-backed hippopotamus
> Rests on his belly in the mud;
> Although he seems so firm to us
> He is merely flesh and blood.

Or as when Queneau begins *Zazie dans le métro* with a word we have to say out loud in order to make sense of it: 'Doukipudonktan' (roughly: 'Where's this stink coming from?').

In the end we have to remember that Bartleby's is an extreme case, or rather, that both the novella, *Bartleby*, and the short story, 'The Hunger Artist', while needing to be taken very seriously, are fictions, ways in which their respective authors manage (as great artists always do) to have their cake and eat it (we saw this at work already in Cervantes' Prologue to *Don Quixote*). My point is that certain ways of writing or painting or composing 'are not possible any more' because they are worn out, thin, lacking in interest, as well as because there are certain things we are not capable of doing any more. In one of the brief passages which go to make up his posthumous book, *On Certainty*, Wittgenstein says: 'Certain events would put me into a position in which I could not go on with the old language-game any further. In which I was torn away from the *sureness* of the game. Indeed, doesn't it seem obvious that the possibility of a language-game is conditioned by certain facts?' This sounds wonderfully clear. The old language-game cannot be played any more because the circumstances have changed, and those who are not aware of this are the enemies of true thought. But that does not stop Wittgenstein, in this so typical of the greatest Modernists, struggling, in the Preface to the *Philosophical Investigations*, with the conundrum of whether he has written the series of fragments which follow because he is, whether through personal weakness or because of the temper of the times, *not up to* writing the kind of large, coherent argument which came naturally to Locke or Kant, or whether he wrote it as a series of fragments *because that is precisely what the argument he was trying to put forward demanded*. Sometimes he thinks it is the one, sometimes the other. There is no-one to tell him which is right. All he knows is that he, being who he is, could have done it in no other way.

III

YESTERDAY, TODAY
AND TOMORROW

13

The Imitation of an Action

What we need is an example of a different language-game. Rabelais, we saw, played his own work off against the Bible, and Cervantes his against *The Odyssey*. Schiller's great essay on the travails of modern art, 'On Naïve and Sentimental Poetry', set the 'naïve' poetry of the ancients against the 'sentimental' or self-conscious poetry of his age. If we are to take an Eliot, a Kafka or a Wittgenstein seriously, then we need to try and focus on a period in which there was no 'dissociation of sensibility', in which Alexander's sword did point the way to his goal, in which there was a 'sureness' about the language-game being played.

Could Greek tragedy provide us with our example? Kierkegaard certainly thought so, for one of the key essays in *Either/Or* is the essay, in Part I, entitled 'The Ancient Tragical Motif as Reflected in the Modern', in which he seeks to bring out the essential difference between ancient and modern tragedy. Our age is more melancholy than that of the Greeks, and so more in despair, says Kierkegaard. The reason for this is that today each person is deemed to be entirely responsible for his actions while 'the peculiarity of ancient tragedy is that the action does not issue exclusively from character, that the action does not find its sufficient explanation in subjective reflection and decision'. We can see this in the very form of ancient and of modern tragedy. Modern tragedy, like all modern drama, proceeds by means of dialogue; in ancient Greek drama dialogue formed only one component of the play, alongside monologue and, above all, the chorus. 'The chorus', says Kierkegaard, 'indicates ... the more which will not be absorbed in individuality.' (And this, incidentally, explains why opera, as Kierkegaard demonstrates in the previous essay in the volume, on Mozart's *Don Giovanni*, can say so much more than drama – music, in opera, has taken over the role of the chorus in ancient Greek drama.)

What is this 'more'? Why does it define ancient tragedy? And why is it absent from its modern counterpart?

> The reason for this naturally lies in the fact that the ancient world did not have subjectivity fully self-conscious and reflective. Even if the individual moved freely, he still rested in the substantial categories of state, family and destiny. This substantial category is exactly the fatalistic element in Greek tragedy, and its exact peculiarity. The hero's destruction is, therefore, not only the result of his own deeds, but it is also, suffering, whereas in modern tragedy, the hero's destruction is really not suffering, but is action.

The hero of Greek tragedy was not an autonomous individual. He was caught in and made by a whole web of different interpenetrating elements. These were what led to tragedy but also what absolved him from full responsibility. Terrible things might happen to him, but he could not blame himself, or, to put it in terms of Greek tragedy itself, he might be polluted but he was not guilty. In modern tragedy, on the other hand, 'the hero stands and falls entirely on his own acts'. 'Our age has lost all the substantial categories of family, state and race. It must leave the individual entirely to himself, so that in a stricter sense he becomes his own creator, his guilt is consequently sin, his pain remorse; but this nullifies the tragic.' For the Greeks, 'life-relationships are once and for all assigned to them, like the heaven under which they live. If this is dark and cloudy, it is also unchangeable.' And, argues Kierkegaard, this is what gives Greek tragedy its soothing quality. It is, he says, surprisingly but acutely, like a mother's love, whereas modern tragedy, where the whole burden is placed on the responsibility of the hero, is (like the father, he implies) ethical, cold and harsh. Tragedy leads to sorrow, ethics to pain. 'Where the age loses the tragic', he concludes, 'it gains despair.'

Early on he makes a vitally important point which, like so much else in his essay, it is easy to pass over at first reading. He has been talking about the chorus and he says: 'In ancient tragedy the action itself has an epic moment in it; it is as much event as action.' To grasp fully what he means by 'an epic moment' and to show how what he is saying here and elsewhere in his essay can help us understand the nature of Modernism, we need to turn from Kierkegaard to another remarkable study of Greek tragedy which has not received its due, a book written by an Oxford English don trained in the law, John Jones. The book, written in 1962, is entitled *On Aristotle and Greek Tragedy*. Surprisingly, Jones, who seems to have read everything, makes no mention of Kierkegaard's essay, but his book can and should be seen as a more scholarly and sustained attempt to tease out its implications.

Jones begins with a chapter on Aristotle's *Poetics*, arguing that we have misread this seminal text because we have been obsessed with the notion, quite alien to Aristotle, of the Tragic Hero. Aristotle, as Kierkegaard had noted, subordinates character to action: 'Tragedy is an imitation not of human beings', says Aristotle, 'but of action and life.' It is the *mimesis* of a *praxis*, the imitation of an action. Jones demonstrates how nineteenth-century translators of the *Poetics*, though many of them were notable scholars, consistently mistranslated it because their (essentially Romantic) world view led them to read into Aristotle what was not there. Take, for instance, the Aristotelian notion of the plays showing us a change of fortune from good to bad.

> The truth is, they are unable to ask themselves whether Aristotle means what he says; they are prevented by an almost invulnerable habit of mind which discredits the *situational* autonomy of [Aristotle's] 'change of fortune', forces a kind of human dependency on it, attaches it to the heroic, suffering solitary who is supposed to stand at the centre of the stage and of attention, like Hamlet.

Jones shows how this affects every decision the translator has to make and how a series of local choices leads in the end to the creation of a quite unreal figure, the Tragic Hero, more Lear than Oedipus, more Lady Macbeth than Clytemnestra (actually more a Romantic *reading* of Lear and Lady Macbeth and Hamlet than a truly Shakespearian one).

This does not of course mean that Aristotle does not imagine that tragedy deals with human beings. 'Aristotle's treatise begins and ends, as any sane aesthetic might, with art confronting life in an effort of interpretation', Jones sensibly remarks. Yet tragedy is not the imitation of *human beings*, it is the imitation of an *action* which involves human beings. As Kierkegaard points out, we tend to think of action as issuing from the solitary consciousness, 'secret, inward, interesting'. For us action is adjectival, it tells us something about character. But, says Jones, 'to our sense of characteristic conduct Aristotle opposes that of characterful action'. Drama based on this view will have no notion of Hamlet's 'I have that within which passes show', because in it a person 'is significantly himself only in what he says and does'. That is why Greek drama is essentially a masked drama. To us moderns a mask hides something, to the Greeks it revealed. 'Masking', says Jones, incidentally revealing that the good critic must be an etymologist, a psychologist, an anthropologist and someone with his finger on the pulse of the present, 'flourishes in totemistic societies – the mask, like the wooden body of the totem, shows forth the psychophysical and institutional solidarity of the descent group'. And masked drama implies that what we see enacted before us is not a fiction or a reconstruction, but in some sense a re-enactment: 'What was done by the man in the story is done again by the mask.' For 'the actor-mask is not a portrait; it presents, it does not represent; it gives us King Oedipus.'

In the light of these remarks, Jones goes on, in the bulk of his book, to analyse the plays of the three tragedians whose work has come down to us. He brings out how little we will understand the *Oresteia* of Aeschylus, the oldest of the three, unless we realise that it is first and foremost not about individuals but about the house (*oikos*) of Atreus (as we still speak of 'the House of Windsor'). The *oikos* consists of 'house and household, building and family, land and chattels, slaves and domestic animals, hearth and ancestral grave: a psycho-physical community of the living and the dead and the unborn'. It is on this house that the lookout stands to speak the opening lines of the play; it is to this hearth that Agamemnon returns; it is the physical wealth of the house that Clytemnestra tempts him to trample underfoot as she begs him to walk on a richly woven carpet; it is the house that suffers a blow as Agamemnon is cut down; the house that is restored as Orestes avenges his father's murder. We make a great mistake, Jones points out, to try and make the carpet symbolic; it is part of our mistaken search for what lies *behind*, instead of focusing on what lies *before* us. The carpet is precious, a lot of work has gone into it, to tread on it is to despoil the house – that is enough.

Similarly, we must take care not to see Agamemnon's dilemma at Aulis as a struggle between King and Father, a conflict between duty and feeling; he has a duty to *both* his positions: as commander of the fleet he has a duty to sacrifice his daughter if that will allow the fleet to sail; as father he has a duty to protect her, as a member of his family, his *oikos*. Nor should we see Clytemnestra as being motivated in the first place by jealousy of Cassandra or lust for Aegisthus. Aeschylus presents her as simply a threat to the *oikos*, a perverter of the natural order of things. When Orestes is about to kill her, in the second play in the trilogy, he says he will kill her next to Aegisthus, 'for he is the man you love and you hate that other whom you were bound to love'. Jones comments: 'When he says that Klytemnestra was bound to love Agamemnon Orestes does not mean that she should have striven to ensure a feeling of love in herself, but that she should have conformed to the love-situation in which she was placed.' This of course brings out how difficult it is in our post-Enlightenment age to make sense of these plays and how our response to art can never be completely separated from our response to the world: we are outraged at the thought of arranged marriages and our individualised society cannot make sense of a term like *philia*, which does not mean romantic love but, as Jones puts it, clumsily as he admits, 'a state of nearness and dearness' – my wife is *philia* to me, but so are my cattle and my spear. Though this may be offensive to us, unless we are prepared to make the imaginative leap we will always simply project our own world picture onto that of other cultures and remain locked up in ourselves, and so deeply impoverished.

Without the music and the choreography we are of course left with a shell of what the Athenian audience would have experienced. Nevertheless, it is possible, with a sensitive masked production like Peter Hall's at the National in 1981, to understand why Kierkegaard should have felt that witnessing these terrible plays is strangely soothing. As Jones puts it: 'The Necessity that crushes a man also vindicates the world's sense.' The tearing of the fabric of the House of Atreus which we witness also brings home to us the strength and resilience of that fabric, and the nourishing virtues of the world's order.

In Aeschylus that order is displayed through the medium of the *oikos*; in Sophocles we move from family to place and from household to person. 'No question of Sophocles' superiority arises', notes Jones, 'but merely of his difference.' The key to Sophocles, he suggests, is his empathy with blindness – the blind Tiresias, the blind Oedipus. Very beautifully, he says:

> All men . . . are teleologically blind. All life moves within a shell-like containment of final ignorance and impotence. To act or think in self-founded certainty of what tomorrow will bring is to ape the poor blind mad man who throws away his stick, shakes off the guiding hand and plunges forward alone. Humanity's stick is its ritual life . . . The guiding hand is lent by the gods.

And death, for Sophoclean man, is not the end-point of life; rather it is that which surrounds humanity like a sea, and men feel this rather as the blind Oedipus feels the sunlight on his body. In a passage which could almost have been written by Kierkegaard, Jones notes:

> In both Aeschylus and Sophocles, the moment when a man perceives the operation of the powers that are destroying him is one of solemn religio-tragic exaltation – not because the individual is 'saved' thereby, but because Necessity and Fate and the ways of Zeus have been exposed for human consciousness in a flash of perfect clarity . . . While Death is terrible, it is also Deliverer and Healer.

Oedipus, after all, performs the task the city has asked of him, that of finding the murderer of Laius and thus cleansing the city of pollution; that this means cleansing the city of himself is terrible for him and his family and sad for the citizens, but it is the price that has to be paid if the city is to survive. His objective pollution and his subjective innocence, explains Jones,

> are features, so to speak, of the tragic mask, visible side by side. Their non-communication is not mysterious, it is the norm of

the Greek masked drama. The mystery is created by ourselves when we seek to validate them in depth, bending them back so that they converge upon a single stable seat of consciousness . . . Instead of which they lie calmly printed on the mask.

Even at the moment of death the two do not come together. In *Oedipus at Colonus* Oedipus, when the thunder sounds, knows what it is he has to do and 'he begins to move with mysterious confidence towards his place of death', as Jones says, a representative of 'all humanity at the dark limit of life, blind, committed to action (there is no doing nothing in Greek tragedy), with a god leading'.

Before that he speaks to his daughters:

My children, this day you lose your father; here and now there perishes all that is I, and you will not any longer bear the burden of tending me – a heavy burden, my children, as I know. And yet one word, quite alone, resolves all this pain. That word is love. Love was the gift you had from me as from no one else, and now you must live out your lives without me. (ll.1611–19)

Jones's comment on this, in its precision and non-sentimentality, suggests why some of us consider him the best English critic of the second half of the twentieth century:

What renders innocent – sanctifies even – Oedipus's thought of his own love lightening his daughters' labours on his behalf, is an obscure literal acceptance of the work which the one little word has been doing; he is not using the word solely to denote the fact of his love, he is looking at the word as at a half-domesticated life which remains still outward and alien at the moment of appropriation. For utterance *is* appropriation: the word *is* Oedipus's.

The effect, he rightly says, 'is a brilliant impenetrability; groping for the people whose words these are, we explore the hard surface of the mask in its linguistic and acoustic dimension'. In other words, we have to learn to live with such impenetrability, to relax and savour it. For it is very precious.

It is the mask that becomes redundant in the exhilarating but perverse plays of the last dramatist of the group, Euripides. For Jones, Euripides arouses the same feelings of an art form in decline, he says, as listening to Beethoven would arouse in a lover of Bach and Haydn. Here at last we find the solitary and inward self of nineteenth-century translations of Aristotle. In *Iphigeneia in Aulis*, for example, we have an Agamemnon who hesitates and changes his mind. First he decides to disband the army; then, persuaded by Menelaus, he alters course and writes a letter (yes, we are finally on familiar dramatic territory) to Clytemnestra, bidding her bring Iphigeneia to Aulis so that she can be married to Achilles (a ruse to get her to come of course). When the play opens he is composing a new letter, having changed his mind once again, telling his wife to keep their daughter at home. At this moment a herald enters to announce that Clytemnestra and Iphigeneia have landed. But Euripides isn't done with us yet. Menelaus now tells his brother that *he* has been persuaded by him and is abandoning his former standpoint: 'Let the army be disbanded and leave Aulis.' But it is too late. Agamemnon points out that Calchas the seer will tell the army about the divine demand for Iphigeneia's life. Menelaus suggests they kill him, but Agamemnon replies that Odysseus too knows about the oracle. There is no escape.

The focus on the inward thus leads to the development of plot, the manipulation by the dramatist of the audience through the introduction of unexpected twists and reversals. In *Iphigeneia in Tauris* Euripides develops the legend that Agamemnon's daughter was transported by Artemis at the moment of sacrifice to the Asian land of Aulis and a deer put in her place. Iphigeneia is now the priestess of Artemis and in charge of sacrificing to her any Athenian youth found in the land. Orestes and Pylades, who have come to Tauris to steal the statue of Artemis, are discovered and brought before Iphigeneia to be sacrificed. The first half of the play ends with brother and sister eventually recognising each other. This would have been enough to fill a whole play by the two older dramatists, but for Euripides it is just the start. The second half consists of the successful carrying out of the plot hatched by Iphigeneia to get all three of them *and* the statue out of Tauris and *en route* to Athens.

This is more like the kind of play we are used to. Not just because seventeenth- and eighteenth-century dramatists and opera librettists turned more often to Euripides than to the other two, but because it's more like the kind of drama we see coming out of Hollywood and on our television screens every night. How exactly does it differ from Aeschylus and Sophocles? First of all, there is no longer any need for the mask. Indeed, masking is a positive hindrance, since so much in these plays turns on the contrast between appearance and reality, or on the nuances of doubt and uncertainty. Jones puts it this way: Sophoclean privacy has been replaced by Euripidean inwardness, which gives us our modern category of the subjective. 'When Orestes saw the Furies in the *Oresteia*', he says, 'he was not experiencing an hallucination: he was polluted. But when the Euripidean Orestes *thought he saw* the Furies (*Orestes*, 408), he knew that his guilty 'conscience' (396) lay at the back of the apparition. At the same time Euripides' new interest in human beings and his new fascination with plot brings with it a failing confidence in *praxis*, action. This is what Kierkegaard was after when he said: 'In ancient tragedy the action itself has an epic moment in it; it is as much event as action.' What he meant was that in the *Agamemnon* or the *Oedipus at Colonus* we witness essentially a single event: the return home and murder of Agamemnon; the arrival at Colonus and going to his death of Oedipus. It unfolds slowly before us, each moment having the same weight as every other; when the event has been explored from all sides, as it were, the play is over, leaving us with that double experience of pity and sorrow, calmness and joy, which Kierkegaard and Jones explore so well. In *Iphigeneia in Tauris*, on the other hand, as in most of Euripides, as in the modern drama against which Jarry, Brecht, Beckett and Ionesco were reacting, we witness the author's manipulation of plot to create exciting theatre, driving towards its (surprising and often unexpected) conclusion. 'Clearly defined terminal climax, so impressively absent in the older drama', concludes Jones, 'becomes a felt need in Euripides.'

What has all this to do with Modernism? Well, if I'm right and Modernism is a response to the simplifications of the self and of life which Protestantism and the Enlightenment brought with them, in return of course for many impressive achievements, then it has everything to do with it. In Euripides we can see emerging precisely those elements that were to form the pillars of art from the Renaissance on: an emphasis on the subjective self and on complicated plotting; a new emphasis on realism; a fascination with those on the margins of society; and a replacement of the sense that it is what we do that defines us by the notion that it is who and what we are that does so. Of course Euripides' work is only symptomatic, one example among many, but, as Nietzsche understood, these transitions happen many times in the history of a culture. We could have looked at Plato and his overturning of the Homeric ethos, as Eric Havelock has done in his brilliant *A Preface to Plato*; or at the way St Paul subverts the Jewish tradition he claims to be upholding, as I tried to do in my book on the Bible. But the contrast of Euripides with the other two tragedians of ancient Athens whose work has come down to us helps us to see some of the elements that make up the Modernist enterprise and what it is struggling against in a fresh light. And if there are other exemplary moments in what we might, in a convenient shorthand, call the transition from privacy to subjectivity, there are also many other examples of what we have found in the older Greek tragedy, some of them much closer to us in both time and space.

In Book III of the *Iliad* Helen, looking down from the walls of Troy at the Greek army assembled below, searches in vain for her two brothers, Castor and Pollux, 'but the two marshallers of the host can I not see', she says,

> Castor, tamer of horses, and the goodly boxer Polydeuces, even mine own brethren, whom the same mother bore. Either they followed not with the host from lovely Lacedaemon, or though they followed hither in their seafaring ships, they have now no heart to enter into the battle of warriors for fear of the words of shame and the many revilings that are mine. (III, 236–42)

'So she said', says the narrator. 'But', he goes on, explaining the real reason why she does not see them, 'they ere now were fast holden of the life-giving earth there in Lacedaemon, in their dear native land' (243–4). They do not appear not because they are ashamed to fight, given what their sister has done, as she imagines, but because they are dead. Except that the poet does not quite say that, he says that the earth, which is the giver of life, now holds them in its embrace; and not anywhere, but in the one place where everyone wants to be buried, their dear native land, 'lovely Lacedaemon'. The effect, as Kierkegaard and Jones said of Greek tragedy, is at once immensely sad and deeply satisfying. A rhythm is asserted which encompasses both Helen and her brothers, life and death, seen as part of the one thing.

This remarkable laconic mode of writing, which is so moving precisely because it eschews the psychological, can also be found much nearer to our own time. Take these central stanzas from one of the greatest of the Border Ballads, that wonderful body of work which flourished in the North of England and the Scottish Lowlands in the fifteenth and sixteenth centuries, 'The Ballad of Sir Patrick Spens':

> 'Mak haste, mak haste, my mirry men all,
> Our guid schip sails the morne';
> 'O say na sae, my master deir,
> For I fear a deadlie storme.
>
> Late late yestreen I saw the new moone,
> With the auld moone in hir arme,
> And I feir, my deir master,
> That we will cum to harme.'
>
> O our Scot nobles wer right laith
> To weet their cork-heild schoone;
> But lang owre a' the play wer playd
> Their hats they swam aboone.
>
> O lang lang may their ladies sit,
> Wi thair fans into their hand,
> Or eir they se Sir Patrick Spens
> Cum sailing to the land.

A terse exchange sets the scene and conveys that sense of foreboding which is a central element in these ballads; and then in one extraordinary stanza everything happens: we first see the fastidious Scottish nobles high-stepping to keep their shoes dry as the sea starts to cover the decks (but that bit is not stated, we have already been given all the information we need to imagine it), then a mere two lines are required to describe, from some position outside both human time and space, the whole expedition and the storm as a cosmic play or game, and to present us with the stark image of the noblemen's hats afloat on the water, the only remaining sign of the ship and its occupants. Finally, as in the biblical Song of Deborah, we switch to the wives and mothers waiting for the men to return, but waiting, of course, in vain.

Something of this doublenesss of vision is what we experience at the key moment in both Golding's *Pincher Martin* and Spark's *The Hothouse by the East River*: a nightmare has come to an end, and if the end is death, the annihilation of the self, then it is also a blessed release from the effort of having to cling on to a lie. Golding, in his early novels, is adept at making us feel what Jones, talking of Sophocles, described as the envelope of life, the sense that we who were at the centre of this nervous bundle of emotions called the self are made to recognize that there exists a life outside us which is utterly other than us. That recognition is, as in Aeschylus and Sophocles, heart-rending, but it is also, in a strange way, healing.

Nowhere is it more terrible than in the last chapter and a half of *The Inheritors*. It is now accepted as probable that it was our human ancestors who put paid to Neanderthal Man. Golding, remarkably, explores this transition from the point of view of the Neanderthalers. For the bulk of the book we are with them, in their simplified, innocent world, a world much more akin to that of animals in its reliance on instinct and inability to grasp agency and causality. We are with them, or rather, with a particular group of them, as their world slowly comes to an end, destroyed by the human beings who have, unfortunately for them, started to live at the edges of their territory, and who, unlike them, have mastered the use of the bow and arrow. In retrospect we realise that the very first episode, in which one of the Neanderthalers falls into the water, catches cold and dies, is not a chance event in the life of the group: he falls into the water because the log that used to lie across it has been removed by the 'new men'. But when, for ten and a half chapters, we have been inside the heads of the Neanderthalers as they slowly succumb, what follows comes as a shock:

> The red creature stood on the edge of the terrace and did nothing. The hollow log was a dark spot on the water towards the place where the sun had gone down. The air in the gap was clear and blue and calm. There was no noise at all now except for the fall, for there was no wind and the green sky was clear. The red creature turned to the right and trotted slowly towards the far end of the terrace ... It was peering down into the thunderous waters but there was nothing to be seen but the columns of glimmering haze where the water had scooped a bowl out of the rock. It moved faster, broke into a queer loping run that made the head bob up and down and the forearms alternate like the legs of a horse ... It put up a hand and scratched under its chinless mouth ... The red creature, now grey and blue in the twilight, loped down the slope and dived into the forest ... It was a strange creature, smallish and bowed. The legs and thighs were bent and there was a whole thatch of curls on the outside of the legs and the arms ... There was no bridge to the nose and the moon-shadow of the jutting brow lay just above the tip. The shadows lay most darkly in the caverns above its cheeks and the eyes were invisible in them. Above this again, the brow was a straight line fledged with hair; and above that there was nothing.

Golding has waited till this point to describe his protagonists from the outside, and the shock is as great as the one produced by Pincher Martin's discovery that there is a congruence between his tooth and his island. For we who have been living and suffering with them are suddenly dragged over to the point of view of the inheritors, the new men, who are set to wipe these red animals from the earth. There is no pathos, no sentimentality. Just the crossover. But it is as powerful as the messenger's speech in *Oedipus at Colonus*.

The double vision need not be so extreme. *A La Recherche* is full of little jolts as the fabric of life which envelops us is momentarily felt and we recognise that we are not the centre of the universe.

Some of these are extremely painful, cannot perhaps ever be quite got over, as when Marcel's mother will not come up to kiss him goodnight or he understands that his grandmother is truly dead, or that Albertine has left him. Swann, in a similar situation, many years before, had, in the end, shrugged his shoulders and muttered something about having wasted the best years of his life with someone who was not his type. Marcel, more open, more curious, more intelligent, more resilient perhaps, works his way down through the pain until the experience is transformed into the joy of his final understanding of our human condition.

The imitation not of human beings but of an action, said Aristotle; and both Kierkegaard and Jones have enabled us to grasp what that implies. This can help us understand not just Aeschylus and Sophocles, but Alain Robbe-Grillet, Claude Simon and Marguerite Duras, those very different writers who came into prominence in the late 1950s and early 1960s and were bundled together by clever publishers and lazy journalists into one entity, the *nouveau roman*. All their major novels deal, in Kierkegaard's terms, with events, not with characters or ethics, with something unfolding which lies beyond our immediate understanding, and certainly beyond that of the protagonists, something they are caught up in rather than the plots devised by traditional novelists. *L'Herbe*, *L'Amante anglaise* and *Le Voyeur* have nothing to do with Greek tragedy except for this central similarity, that they deal with the event seen in its epic dimension and not with plotting or character, though of course it is characters we can relate to who 'carry' the action. Consequently endings cease to have the importance that they do in the classic novel; as with Pinget's *Passacaille*, a field is thoroughly tilled and, when that is done, the work ends. Not that there is no tension in these works, or that we have no urge to turn the pages – just as we watch the plays of Aeschylus and Sophocles with rapt attention till the final chorus is done – but that it is a very different experience from wondering whether Orestes and Iphigeneia will succeed in making their escape from Tarsus.

Seeing the art of the twentieth century in the light of the ancient Greek stage can help us to understand many things. Why, for example, Gert Hofmann and Agota Kristof chose to write in the first person plural, or why the attitude of so many artists to the objects they chose to depict changed radically from what it had been in earlier times. Kafka's first diary entry, for example, dated 1910, describes an event and not a person or even a group of people: 'The onlookers go rigid when the train goes past (*Die Zuschauer erstarren, wenn der Zug vorbeifährt*).' Kafka is interested not in the people on the station platform and not in the train but in what-happens-when-the-train-goes-rushing-past. Writing about his 1911 painting of a coffee mill, Duchamp puts it very clearly: 'Instead of making an objective, figurative coffee-grinding machine, I did a description of the mechanism. You see the cogwheel and you see the turning handle at the top, with an arrow showing the direction in which it turned, so there was the idea of movement.' The depiction of movement, which is such an obsession with Duchamp and which can be seen to lie behind such early filmic masterpieces as René Clair's *Entr'acte* and Dziga Vertov's *Man with a Movie Camera*, is not the result of artists' obsession with the new and faster means of travel appearing at the time, as positivist historians assert; those means of travel, as well as the possibilities of film, rather, help artists return to those older principles of art: the imitation not of character but of action.

Both Picasso and Stravinsky turned, at crucial moments in their lives, to the art of ancient Greece. Both did so very successfully because their work had always been in secret sympathy with it rather than with that of the majority of their contemporaries. The Greece they went back to was not that to which earlier ages had gone back, and though they could produce 'classical' work, *Apollon Musagète* or the illustrations to Ovid's *Metamorphoses*, these were never inert pastiches, but held within invisible inverted commas, so to speak, and were revitalised by wit. But they are not ultimately what is most important in the *oeuvre* of both artists. The Ovid was produced in 1930, and in the course of that decade Picasso immersed himself in a very different Greece, perhaps alerted to it by Bataille and his journal *Documents*, but explored in such depth because it corresponded to his own vision in those years. Here, indeed, what he goes back to is the Minotaur, the labyrinth, the violence at the heart of the preclassical – but always held in compositions of precision and wit. Picasso, as we have seen, was determined to avoid both abstraction and mechanisation. As Leo Steinberg has shown, his intense concentration on

Delacroix's *Women of Algiers* in the immediate post-war years was fed by the desire to be at once in there with the women and outside, seeing them not as exotic creatures but, as Aeschylus and Sophocles had seen their protagonists, as human beings caught like all of us in the web of life and circumstances. In the last version, as Steinberg shows, Picasso finally gets everything right, and as he does so he finds himself, as so often with great artists, returning to a theme he had not thought about when he started on this particular project but which had haunted him for a very long time, the relation of the horizontal and the vertical woman to each other in two-dimensional space.

As for Stravinsky, his dialogue with the past goes back to his first ballets, though it was perhaps only with *Pulcinella* that he became conscious of what this involved. '*Pulcinella* was my discovery of the past', he later wrote, 'the epiphany through which the whole of my late work became possible. It was a backward look, of course – the first of many love affairs in that direction – but it was a look in the mirror too.' And then, echoing Eliot's 'Bad poets imitate, good poets steal': 'People who had never heard of, or cared about, the originals, cried "sacrilege": "The classics are ours. Leave the classics alone." To them all my answer was and is the same: You "respect", but I love.' Stravinsky collaborated with Cocteau on his oratorio, *Oedipus Rex* (1927), but, as he told Robert Craft later, Cocteau, with his superficial love of the 'dramatic', became an embarrassment. Stravinsky instinctively sensed the monumental qualities of the play, its subordination of character to fate, and where Cocteau, in his interspersed narration ('Il tombe. Il tombe de haut'), tries to milk the pathos of Oedipus' tragic discovery that he is the polluter, Stravinsky's music wonderfully keeps alive Sophocles' sense that if this is a disaster for Oedipus it is nonetheless the salvation of the city of Thebes.

Stravinsky is attuned to the double movement of Greek tragedy, its ability to show personal disaster and a kind of comfort coexisting in *Oedipus Rex*, because that is how he had seen things from the start. *Le Sacre du printemps* is so powerful because it recognises that the renewal of the earth can only come at the cost of sacrifice – it recognises it in the 'scenario', but even more in the music, whose pounding rhythms are at once a sign of doom and of renewal. Yet it is perhaps in *Les Noces* that this sense of life and of what kind of art is required to body it forth is most fully realised. It is so much greater a work than the many nineteenth-century dramatisations of pastoral peasant weddings because it recognises the enormous *cost* of marriage as well as its enormous rewards. As in all of Stravinsky, plangency and celebration are one, as first the bride's friends mourn the cutting of her hair and her having to leave her family, and then celebrate her entry into a new union, a new home.

As we leave the concert hall where we have witnessed *Les Noces*, we sense that we have experienced an event, a *praxis*, which has renewed our sense of what it means to be human, that it has revealed to us the pain and the joy of life and how the two are inextricably intertwined. But even if there are no masks and no 'stage action' Stravinsky is at pains to remind us that this is not a *praxis*, an action, but an *imitation*, a *mimesis* of an action. Different voices 'speak for' the different protagonists at different times, thus allowing us to identify not with the characters so much as with the action – a device Stravinsky had already used in his wartime pieces such as *Renard*. It is well known too that Stravinsky had enormous difficulty in deciding how to orchestrate the piece. As the war dragged on he tried combination after combination, but nothing would quite answer to his needs. At last, shortly before the first performance in 1923, he hit on what he felt was the right solution: a small orchestra in which four pianos take on the role of the percussion. At the end the four pianos, two crotales and one bell come together in a fortissimo chord. The choir stops. The solo unaccompanied bass chants the opening modal theme in its syncopated form – 'Dear Heart, Dear Wife . . .' The phrases are punctuated by the tolling of the 'bell' chord on every eighth beat. The bass voice dies away and the syncopated theme is taken over by the instruments. A lesser composer (even a fine composer like Messiaen) would have given us church bells. Not Stravinsky. The sound of those four pianos, wonderfully imitating but never pretending to be church bells, is a fitting climax to one of the greatest of all Modernist works.

Since *Oedipus Rex* there have of course been numerous attempts to write operas based on ancient tragedy, from Henze to Birtwistle. Most of these fail because they are essentially taking a nineteenth-century form and trying to accommodate it to ancient modes. They have not learnt the lesson of Stravinsky's radical rethinking of what can constitute music theatre. One composer who has is Luigi Nono, whose *Prometeo*, subtitled 'a tragedy of hearing', was first performed in 1984. We had to wait twenty-four years for it to arrive on these shores: the first English performance took place in London in May 2008.

Nono was a Venetian, much influenced by the spaces of San Marco and the way composers like Monteverdi and Gabrieli used them, but influenced too by his Marxism, his friendships with the other major composers of his time, such as Boulez, Berio, Ligeti and Kurtág, all highly cultured and deeply thoughtful men, and by his wide reading in European literature, especially Hölderlin. He understood that to write a traditional opera today is to court disaster. *Prometeo* has no scene, no stage action and no protagonists. Nono transforms the space in which the piece is to be played into a soundbox in which musicians and audience are both placed. Using fragments of texts from Aeschylus' *Prometheus Unbound*, Hesiod and Sophocles, in Greek, with fragments of Hölderlin and Walter Benjamin, in German, the words broken up into syllables dispersed among the singers, four different orchestral groupings and complicated electronics which make it impossible to locate the source of any of the sounds, he asks us to listen. *Ascolta* (listen) is a word frequently repeated by the singers and which we can pick up out of the web of Greek and German and Italian syllables. To listen properly is what the opera teaches us to do. This means staying in the moment, staying with the long, long silences, calming down our desire for plot and resolution. But this does not mean that the work is abstract, any more than Picasso's 1912 collages were abstract. It deals with Prometheus and with the sufferings of humanity at the hands of cruel gods. But it does not preach any more than the Picasso collages or *The Waste Land* do. Living through the two-and-a-quarter-hour-long experience leaves us, as we are left at the end of *Oedipus at Colonus*, with a sense of sorrow and of wonder and, at an even deeper level, a sense of having bathed in the waters of life.

14

It Took Talent To Lead Art That Far Astray

Here are three quotations:

He spoke sententiously, breaking off abruptly. I had an uneasy feeling, unlikely as this would be, that he might be about to ask me to act as best man at his wedding. I began to think of excuses to avoid such a duty. However, it turned out he had no such intention. It seemed likely, on second thoughts, that he wanted to discuss seriously some matter regarding himself which he feared might, on ventilation, cause amusement.

If it had not been such an intolerably hot evening, Bernard would have suggested remaining in their seats in the interval. He could see no point in a meeting between Eric and Terence, though he had never hidden his relationships from either of them. They would, he felt sure, dislike one another and he dreaded a little his own acquiescence in their criticisms. They would both be so perfectly right, and they would both so perfectly miss the point.

'Jake,' said Madge into my shoulder, 'don't leave me.'
I half carried her to the settee. I felt calm and resolute. I knelt beside her and took her hand, brushing her hair back with my hand. Her face rose towards me like a lifting flower.
'Jake,' said Madge, 'I must have you with me. That was what it was all for. Don't you see?'
I nodded. I drew my hand back over her smooth hair and down to the warmth of her neck.

Each of these extracts, chosen at random, comes from a novel by the writers recommended, back in 1958, by the then Professor of

English at Oxford, Lord David Cecil, as being in the vanguard of fiction writing in English. (Why, I wonder now, did he make no mention of Ivy Compton-Burnett? Probably because, his taste being typical of the English establishment, then and now, he did not rate her.) The first comes from *At Lady Molly's*, by Anthony Powell, published in 1957, the second from *Hemlock and After*, by Angus Wilson, published in 1952, and the third from *Under the Net*, Iris Murdoch's first novel, published in 1954. Occasionally they sound dated, as in Powell's 'which he feared might, on ventilation, cause amusement', or Wilson's 'They would both be so perfectly right, and they would both so perfectly miss the point'. But by and large they have stood the test of time pretty well; or rather, they could have been extracts from novels published in England in 2009. They all three do what they set out to do perfectly adequately: they help tell a story and create a world and characters to inhabit that world that do not flout the laws of probability. We never doubt what they are telling us, whether it is about the way someone speaks ('sententiously'), the weather ('an intolerably hot evening') or an action ('I half carried her to the settee'). It does not matter whether the narrative is in the first or the third person, what the narrator says is, as far as we are concerned, the truth. Such narratives are easy to read. They are also illustrative, in Bacon's sense: they tell a story, they have no life of their own. The two things go together, as both Barthes and Merleau-Ponty showed: the smooth chain of the sentences gives us a sense of security, of comfort even, precisely because it denies the openness, the 'trembling' of life itself; the very confidence of the articulation of the narrative gives the lie to our own sense of things being confused, dark, impossible to grasp fully. That of course is why we read them: they take us, for a while, out of our confusions, drawing us into a world that makes some sort of sense, that at the very least can be articulated. By the same token they cannot really satisfy us, since they do not speak to our condition, only make us hungry for more.

As I hope I have made clear, in my discussions of Cervantes and of Golding, for example, a sense of narrative being alive does not depend on the disruption of syntax or the use of demotic speech, but on a much more fundamental relation of the writer to his medium. If Barthes is right and to be modern is to know that some things can no longer be done, then Cervantes is modern and these writers are not.

And what of their successors? Here again are three extracts, chosen at random, all from living writers. The first comes with an endorsement from Anthony Thwaite ('a prose that has a feline grace'), the second with one from Karl Miller ('the masterpiece of someone I think of as the best novelist writing in England'), and the third with one from John Braine ('a beautifully written story'):

'What is it, Mary?' Colin said, and reached for her hand. She shrank away, but her eyes were on him . . . and he shivered as he fumbled for his shirt and stood up. They faced each other across the empty bed. 'You've had a bad fright,' Colin said, and began to edge round towards her. Mary nodded and moved towards the french window that gave on to the balcony.

She had always seen decay about her, even while going through all that the society asked of her. Slot machines on railway stations were full of sweets, but she knew they would be empty again; they were meant to be empty, as they had been when she was a child, pieces of junk that no one yet thought of taking away.

We had by now descended the long incline of our street and reached Elizabeth Avenue. No lawn we passed, no driveway, no garage, no lampost, no little brick stoop was without its power over me. Here I had practised my sidearm curve, here on my sled I'd broken a tooth, here I had copped my first feel, here for teasing a friend I had been slapped by my mother, here I had learned that my grandfather was dead.

It is clear, again, that all three passages have more in common than they have differences. One may employ dialogue, one what linguists call *style indirecte libre*, and one a first person narrator, but all three are concerned with telling a story and telling it in such a way as to make readers feel that they are not reading about a world that has been freshly made but about one that has always existed. Writing in the 1950s about the Citroën DS 19, Barthes pointed out: 'It is obvious that the new Citroën has fallen from the sky inasmuch as it appears at first sight as a superlative object'. It is characterised, he goes on, at once by 'a perfection and an absence of origin, a closure and a brilliance, a transformation of life into matter'. A recent commentator on this essay adds: 'One of the most noteworthy features of the car was its lack of noticeable joints; its panels were not visibly riveted, they appeared to coexist in a state of magical juxtaposition. That is to say, the tangible signs of fabrication, of the labor expended in transforming raw matter into consummable object, had been magicked away.' Like the Citroen DS 19, the works from which I have just quoted (like the earlier ones of Powell, Wilson and Iris Murdoch) are carefully made objects, exquisitely crafted in order to conceal the joints. The price they pay for this is that they are thin, illustrative, again, in Bacon's sense, recounting anecdotes which may or may not hold our attention but to which we certainly would not want to return, since they lack that sense of density of other worlds suggested but lying beyond words, which we experience when reading Proust or James or Robbe-Grillet. We read them to pass the time, to reassure ourselves that the world has meaning, and then we leave them and move on to the next book.

The first is by a Booker Prize winner, the second by a Nobel Prize winner, and the third is – by Philip Roth. But surely, you may say, Philip Roth is an experimental writer! He writes novels in which a character called Philip Roth appears; he writes novels with titles like *The Counterlife*, which play with the notion of possible other worlds. Is that not what Modernism is about?

If that is your reaction you have not really been taking in what I have been saying. Cervantes may suddenly suspend his narrative and go on to tell us that the manuscript broke off at this point; Proust may later reveal that what had been said earlier was wrong, and then later still that this new revelation was itself wrong. But it is not these things that make their novels modern. It is partly that they hunger for that 'relentless contact' which so haunted Stevens's Comedian and for a form of fiction which transcends the anecdotal – the dreariness of 'the marquise went out at five' – so that they are unwilling to settle for that fixed distance from the language they are using and the story they are telling, which is such a feature of the English writers I have just been looking at; and partly (the two are of course interconnected) that they understand that, in Wittgenstein's words, a certain language-game can no longer be played, and that this does not mean that we can simply shift the ground and find another language-game to play. For all Philip Roth's playfulness (a heavy-handed playfulness at the best of times), he never doubts the validity of what he is doing or his ability to find a language adequate to his needs. As a result his works may be funny, they may be thought-provoking, but only as good journalism can be funny and thought-provoking. Those of us who cannot find the words to make sense of our lives may look on in admiration but not feel, as we feel with Sophocles or Duras, that this speaks to us.

Writers of course only do what they can. They instinctively sense, or quite soon work out, what they can and can't do, and what they want and do not want to do (the two are not always the same). Even Dickens, that most self-assured of novelists, provides, in *The Pickwick Papers*, a fascinating glimpse into all the directions in which he thought for a moment he might go but in the end decided (not consciously, I'm sure) not to explore. *Don Quixote* hovers over the whole book of course, as it does not over later Dickens, and in Chapter 11 we even find him flirting with two of Poe's favourite genres, Gothic horror (the inset story of the madman's confessions) and the decipherment by the rational mind of a mysterious inscription. His comic take on the latter is evidence both of the English novel's robust common sense, its refusal to be taken in by the pseudo-profound, and of Dickens' rueful acknowledgement that the direction of Poe, Hawthorne and Melville can never be his. But if writers do what they are drawn to do, critics and cultural analysts need to do a little better. It is not Powell, Wilson and Murdoch, not our current Booker and Nobel Prize winners who give cause for concern, but the cultural climate that cannot see the difference between them and those writers who, in Kierkegaard's terms, sense vividly what is lacking and then endeavour to convey a sense of this lack, between works that illustrate and works that live.

An interesting example of our current confusions is the reception recently accorded to Irène Némirovsky's *Suite Française*. Némirovsky was a Russian-born Jew living in France who wrote in French. The book was written in 1941–2, shortly before its author was deported and murdered. The manuscript surfaced in the early 1990s (it had been lying in her daughter's trunk all the time) and was published to some acclaim in France, but to nothing like the rapturous reception it received in Britain. Doris Lessing and the journalist Robert Fisk compared it to Tolstoy, and Victoria Glendinning, the distinguished biographer, described it as one of the most significant books of the last century.

The first part deals with the fall of France in May 1940 and the subsequent exodus from Paris. Here is an extract from the first pages:

> In the Péricand household they listened in shocked silence to the evening news on the radio, but no one passed comment on the latest developments. The Péricands were a cultivated family; their traditions, their way of thinking, their middle-class, Catholic background, their ties with the Church (their eldest son Philippe Péricand was a priest), all these things made them mistrustful of the government of France. On the other hand Monsieur Péricand's position as curator of one of the country's national museums bound them to an administration that showered its faithful with honours and financial rewards.
>
> A cat held a little piece of bony fish tentatively between its sharp teeth, he was afraid to swallow, but he couldn't bring himself to spit it out either.
>
> Madame Péricand finally decided that only a male mind could explain with clarity such strange, serious events.

Némirovsky was a popular novelist of the day and she uses the clichés of the middlebrow novel without embarrassment, quickly filling in the background and sketching in her chosen representative family with the minimum of fuss, then cutting to the cat so as to convey the sense of ordinary life going on regardless of the great events that are unfolding. 'The Péricands were', 'a cat held' – we remember how Proust felt the chill of death enveloping him when he came across such a use of the past tense in Sainte-Beuve and elsewhere. A story is told and, as in the English extracts above, everything is done to make sure the inventing author is concealed, but the work lies inert on the page, without any life of its own.

The very poignancy of what happened in France in those days in May 1940 makes such stale narrative retellings all the more grotesque. Will it get better when we reach the actual fighting?

'This is a disaster,' thought Hubert with a sigh. 'This is defeat! I am here, watching an enormous defeat, worse than Waterloo. We are all lost. I'll never see Mother or any of my family again. I'm going to die.' He felt doomed, numb to everything around him, in a terrible state of exhaustion and despair. He didn't hear the order to retreat. He saw men running through the machine-gun fire. Rushing forward, he climbed over a wall into a garden where a baby's pram still stood in the shade. The battle wasn't over. Without tanks, without weapons, without ammunition, they were still trying to defend a few square metres of ground, a bridgehead, while from all directions the German conquerors were sweeping through France.

Though utter chaos is being described, the collapse of a world, Hubert has time to talk to himself in cadenced phrases, to draw comparisons from history. And notice how the baby's pram is conveniently waiting 'in the shade' to make the same sort of point as was made by the description of the cat in the first extract. This is run-of-the-mill middlebrow narrative, given poignancy by the subsequent history of its author and of the manuscript itself. It is this, I feel, that has allowed commentators, who secretly warm to this kind of writing but don't quite dare admit it, to grow ecstatic about the book with a clear conscience: the events it describes were terrible and dramatic, the author's fate was tragic, the fate of the manuscript miraculous, so it must be a great book. Contrast (even in my clumsy translation) a real writer tackling the same subject, Claude Simon's attempt to convey what was engulfing France and its army in that same moment of May 1940, seen through the eyes of a cavalry officer still, unbelievable as it might appear, as in 1914, astride a horse, in the face of the armoured onslaught of the Germans. Through the eyes, though, is wrong, itself a cliché: part of the power of Simon's novel comes from the fact that it is an anguished monologue as the narrator tries to explain to the woman in whose bed he is lying, and to explain to himself, what had just happened:

on this road which was nothing but a death-trap, that is, not war but murder pure and simple, a place where they cut you down before you could say ouch, the snipers calmly installed behind a hedge or a bush and taking all the time in the world to get you into their sights, in short a bloody shooting-gallery . . . which did not stop him from always holding himself stiff and upright in his saddle, as upright as though he'd been reviewing a march past at a 14 July parade and not in the middle of a retreat or rather a rout or rather a disaster in the midst of this kind of decomposition of everything as though not simply an army but the world itself in its entirety and not just its physical reality but the image the mind can make of it (but perhaps it was also the lack of sleep, the fact that for ten days we had practically not slept except in the saddle) . . . two or three times someone shouted out to him not to go on (how many I don't know, nor who they were: the wounded I imagine, or men hidden in the houses or in the ditch, or perhaps civilians who doggedly went on wandering about in incomprehensible fashion, dragging a battered suitcase after them or pushing one of those children's perambulators filled with vague belongings (not really belongings: just things, useless objects, simply no doubt so as not to wander empty-handed, having the illusion of taking with them, of possessing anything so long as it was personal: a torn pillow or an umbrella or the colour photograph of the grandparents – and so had the arbitrary notion of price, of treasure attached to it) as though what mattered was simply to walk, no matter in what direction. . .)

My instinct is to say: the difference between the two descriptions is not one of degree but of kind. It is not that Némirovsky is a lesser novelist than Simon, but that she is simply unaware of the inappropriateness of what she is doing, and one has to say that by her writing she makes 'a written renunciation to all claim to be an author'. Or is this too apocalyptic? Is it simply that she *is* less good, less aware of what can and cannot be done, less aware of just what it is she wants to convey and therefore of the need to forge a style that will answer to that need?

Again, the question is not why she should have written as she did, but what has happened to our culture that serious and intelligent and well-read reviewers, not to speak of prize-winning novelists and distinguished biographers, many of whom have studied the poems of Eliot or the novels of Virginia Woolf at university, should so betray their calling as to go into ecstasies over books like Némirovsky's while, in their lifetimes and now after their deaths, ignoring the work of novelists like Claude Simon, Georges Perec, Thomas Bernhard and Gert Hofmann.

To answer this would require a sociologist, perhaps, and another book. But a few points are worth making. The first is that though, as the example of Némirovsky shows, we are not dealing here with a purely English phenomenon, there is a greater resistance to or lack of awareness of Modernism right across the board in England than there is in the rest of Europe and even in America. Modernism has its friends over here but they are what the art historian T.J. Clark has called 'false friends', that is, those who defend a version of Modernism that is at once crude and superficial and therefore make it even more difficult to grasp what it truly is. A case in point is a recent book by the young English novelist Adam Thirlwell, *Miss Herbert*, which deals with many of the themes and authors I have been writing about here, but seems (to me) consistently to misrepresent and misunderstand them.

I have already had occasion to quote Thirlwell on *Don Quixote*, which he reads as 'the juxtaposition of chivalrously good intentions with the prose of real life'. This, I suggested, is to misunderstand the questions raised by the novel about truth and authority and especially the authority of the novelist himself. For Cervantes, the question of what is 'real life' and how an artist today (his today and our today) can claim to deal with it is a fundamental concern; for Thirlwell it isn't an issue. Thus his misreading of Cervantes is symptomatic of his whole book. What he takes both the novel and Modernism to stand for, as far as I can see, is an unflinching realism which resolutely refuses the consolations of poetry and Romanticism. He quotes Flaubert: 'I want a touch of bitterness in everything – always a jeer in the midst of our triumphs, desolation even in the midst of enthusiasm', and remarks: 'That last sentence is Flaubert's description of his new literary form: the novelistic scene, the anti-lyrical poem.'

The touchstone of this new form, a form which will at last 'be true to the mess which is real life', is the telling detail: the faint scar on a forehead, the stair carpet turned up at one corner. Thirlwell purrs with pleasure when he finds it in Diderot or Flaubert, in Tolstoy or Nabokov. It is the detail which shows up the impurity of grandiose feelings, which does the job of the novelist and the Modernist, deflating the sentimental, the romantic, the serious. 'The most radical novels find comedy in places which people do not want to see as comic at all – like sex, or concentration camps.' This is meant to be shocking but it is merely in bad taste. For Hitler and the camps seem actually to be immune to comedy, as the films Chaplin and Roberto Benigni devoted to those subjects, *The Great Dictator* and *Life is Beautiful*, merely serve to demonstrate. Even a great comic novel like *Catch-22* only works, as David Daiches once pointed out, because it is set at a moment in the Second World War when the Allied victory was already assured.

The notion that the new reality inhering in novels depends on their attention to detail fails to distinguish between 'reality' and what theoreticians call 'the reality-effect'. In fact Thirlwell uses the two terms indiscriminately. But putting a faint scar on a face or alerting us to the fact that the carpet is turned up in the corner, like describing the smell of sweat and semen during the act of sex, no more anchors the novel to 'reality' than writing about stars in the eyes of the beloved. The novel is still made up of words, is still the product of a solitary individual, inventing scars, carpets, smells or stars. Of course we warm to a novelist who surprises us with his attention to detail, though as much or more depends on the way it is done, the style, rather than the detail itself, as when Dickens has Sam Weller say: 'Look at these here boots – eleven pairs o'boots; and one shoe as b'longs to number six, with the wooden leg', or Proust writes of Swann's arrival at a grand party and the footman's taking his hat and gloves: 'As he approached Swann, he seemed to be exhibiting at once an utter contempt for his person and the most tender regard for his hat.' Too often though, especially in Flaubert and the Goncourts, detail seems to be there as a way of convincing us (and the authors themselves?) that what we are dealing with is the stuff of life. Too often the attention to detail in modern novels reminds me of what Clement Greenberg once said of nineteenth-century academic painting: 'It took talent – among other things – to lead art that far astray. Bourgeois society gave these talents a prescription, and they filled it – with talent.'

Thirlwell's failure to distinguish reality and the 'reality-effect' is symptomatic of his – and his English colleagues' – failure to grasp what was obvious to every artist I have been looking at in the course of this book, that what is at issue is reality itself, what it is and how an art which of necessity renounces all claim to contact with the transcendent can relate to it, and, if it cannot, what possible reason it can have for existing. This is not an issue for Thirlwell. 'The problem of living in Brazil, or Cuba, or Russia, and wanting to write a novel', he says grandly, 'is the same problem as living in France, or Britain, and wanting to write a novel. The problem is universal: it is about finding a way of describing real life.'

Thirlwell and his mentor Craig Raine, for all their waving of Modernist credentials, seem as confident as Jane Austen that the ground they stand on is solid. What I have tried to suggest in the course of this book is that, for some artists at least since the time of Dürer, and for any serious artist since 1789, the ground has been anything but solid. And that if this is the case then it is not enough to examine the surface of a work, to admire the artist's skill in doing this or that. What we need to do is to see it from the point of view of the artist – not of course Picasso or Stravinsky or Eliot the man but the maker. The reason for this is that *the work itself* asks for such a reading. *Don Quixote*, like *Prufrock* or Kafka's 'The New Advocate', is not just 'about' the juxtaposition of romantic beliefs and the world's reality; it recognises itself as implicated in an impossible struggle to reconcile these two, and it implicates the reader.

But our English pseudo-Modernists cannot or will not see this. They pride themselves on their realism, which means their beady-eyed refusal to be taken in by highfalutin language and all the temptations of Romanticism. Love is not about stars in your eyes, it is about the itch of sex; death is not a consummation devoutly to be wished but a dingy and degrading experience; art is there not to make you rejoice but to rub your nose in the dirt. As well as thanking, in the course of his book, his old tutor Craig Raine, Adam Thirlwell thanks Julian Barnes, and Barnes's latest book, *Nothing to be Frightened of*, perfectly exemplifies this mindset. Shocked by the death of his parents and his realisation that, at sixty, he has not all that much time to go himself, Barnes spends 250 pages telling himself and us how frightened he is at the prospect. What is terrifying about old age is the loss of

174 YESTERDAY, TODAY AND TOMORROW

control, and this is particularly difficult for Barnes because he seems to have inherited his mother's need to be in control at all times and never to be taken in by sentiment, though he recognises the ambiguous roots of such feelings. 'I was an idealistic adolescent', he writes, 'who swerved easily into suspicion when confronted with life's realities. My kicks were those of a disheartened Romantic.' This is insightful, but he doesn't follow it up. Rather, he seems happy to accept himself as a clear-eyed realist. 'I hope, Barnes', one of his teachers says to him, 'that you're not one of those bloody back-row cynics.' 'Me, sir? Cynic, sir? Oh no – I believe in baa-lambs and hedgerow blossoms and human goodness, sir', the grown-up Barnes responds across the years. But this kind of smartness soon palls. It's bright but it tries too hard to shock, like the joke which he likes so much he repeats it: 'Alzheimer's? *Forget* it.' Barnes, like Thirlwell and Raine, prides himself on his realism, which he likes to think brings him closer to his beloved Flaubert. But the trouble with this English brand of Realism is that it yields an impoverished view of life and leaves Barnes prey to all the fears he has striven to repress.

Reading Barnes, like reading so many of the other English writers of his generation, Martin Amis, Ian McEwan, Blake Morrison, or a critic from an older generation who belongs with them, John Carey, leaves me feeling that I and the world have been made smaller and meaner. Ah, they will say, but that is just what we wanted, to free you of your illusions. But I don't believe them. I don't buy into their view of life. The irony which at first made one smile, the precision of language, which was at first so satisfying, the cynicism, which at first was used only to puncture pretension, in the end come to seem like a terrible constriction, a fear of opening oneself up to the world. It is sad to see this has infected a writer from the next generation like Adam Thirlwell. All of them ultimately come out of Philip Larkin's overcoat, and clearly their brand of writing and the nature of their vision speaks to the English, for they are among the most successful writers of their generation. I wonder, though, where it came from, this petty-bourgeois uptightness, this terror of not being in control, this schoolboy desire to boast and to shock. We don't find it in Irish or American culture, or in French or German or Italian culture. The English have always been both sentimental and ironical, but there was never that sense of prep-school boys showing off, which is the taste these writers leave on my tongue.

How has it come about? I would venture three points. 'Like most Victorian novelists', writes John Bayley, '[Dickens'] sense of other places and people was founded on fear and distrust. The Boz of the *Sketches* seems to hate and fear almost everything even though it fascinates him.' But this is something that antedates the Victorians. As Linda Colley has shown in her fine book, *Britons*, from the early eighteenth century on Britons defined themselves in opposition to others, in particular to the large, aggressive Popish nations of Spain and France: Britons are different; Britons never will be slaves, to other nations or to the ideas of other nations. To this must be added the fact that England was just about the only European country not to be overrun by enemy forces during the Second World War, which was a blessing for it, but which has left it strangely innocent and thrown it into the arms, culturally as well as politically, of the even more innocent United States. This has turned a robust pragmatic tradition, always suspicious of the things of the mind, into a philistine one. Though there is something appealing in the resolute determination not to be taken in evinced by Larkin and Amis in the face of European Modernism, something that reminds me of the *Just William* books I so enjoyed as a child, it soon begins to pall. Taken as a cultural rallying-cry it is little short of disastrous.

Second, and paradoxically, ours is an age which, while being deeply suspicious of the 'pretentious', worships the serious and the 'profound', so that large novels about massacres in Rwanda or Bosnia, or historical novels with a 'majestic sweep', are automatically considered more worthy of attention than the novels of, say, P.G. Wodehouse or Robert Pinget.

Finally, ours is the first generation in which High Art and Fashion have married in a spirit joyously welcomed by both parties. When the speakers at major *literary* festivals are for the most part politicians, television personalities or foreign correspondents; when we are enjoined to buy three books for the price of two in our major bookshops and a serious newspaper like the *Independent* offers its readers the chance, as a Christmas bonanza, to gatecrash a book launch of their choice with one of the paper's literary critics, we have truly arrived at an age where art and showbiz are one and the same.

In his delightful novel, *Rates of Exchange*, Malcolm Bradbury touches on the first of my points when he has his East European magical realist *femme fatale*, Katya Princip, explain his own history to the bemused British Council lecturer, Dr Petworth:

> Oh, Mr. Petwit, I have told you. You are really not a character in the world historical sense. You come from a little island with water all round. When we were oppressed and occupied and when we fought and died, and there were mad mullahs and pogroms against the Jews, what did you have? Queen Victoria and industrial revolution and Alfred Lord Tennyson. We sent Karl Marx to explain everything, but you didn't notice. What did you do with him? Put him in Highgate cemetery, some would say the best place, I know. You never had history, just some customs.

This is so brilliant because it is at the same time an acute assessment of how England relates to Europe, a sending up of what 'Europe' in this equation stands for, and a covert thumbs up to traditional English ways. For who, reading this, would not opt for customs rather than history, for Queen Victoria and Alfred Lord Tennyson rather than mad mullahs and pogroms? But is that really the choice? You cannot escape from history with a few comic phrases. As historians, not all Marxist, have been pointing out for rather a long time now, naturally Britain has had a history, but it has preferred to ignore that history. Perhaps the best one can say is that it has had the luxury of not having that history thrust upon it as most of the European nations have.

So many English novelists today confess to wanting to write like Dickens that it might be thought that the difference between England and France and Germany is that we have no great model to look back to, who might give us an understanding of what it might mean to have a European sensibility, that is, to be as English as they come and yet have a real historical awareness. But there is one, as I have suggested: Wordsworth. Unfortunately within English culture he has been consistently misrepresented as either a bucolic poet or a political reactionary. This is a travesty. He occupies the same place in English literary history as, say, Hölderlin and Baudelaire occupy in German and French: someone with all the powers of the Romantic poet at his fingertips but aware of the deep paradoxes of his calling in an age when art itself is in question. Wordsworth, James, Eliot and Virginia Woolf all flourished on these shores. We need to go back and try to understand what they were up to *as writers*, not dismiss them as reactionaries or misogynists, or adulate them as gay or feminist icons.

15

Stories Of Modernism

Naturally I think the story I have just finished telling is the true one. At the same time I recognise that there are many stories and that there is no such thing as *the* true story, only more or less plausible explanations, stories that take more or less account of the facts. I am aware too that these stories are *sites of contestation*; more is at stake than how we view the past. That is what is wrong with positivist accounts of Modernism, which purport simply to 'tell the story', like Peter Gay's *Modernism*. These make a show of impartiality but are of course just as partial as any other account.

What I characterised at the start as the prevalent English view, epitomised by Waugh, Larkin and Amis, that Modernism was just a blip in the serene history of the arts, might appear at first sight to be not very different from Gay's position, but it is in fact profoundly different, for it is deeply polemical, even if the polemic is fuelled by anxiety rather than anything else. A slightly more sophisticated version of this is the one espoused by those I have just called, borrowing the term from T.J. Clark, the false friends of Modernism. This sees Modernism, in a very English way, as a Good Thing because it debunks Romanticism and idealism. Modernism, according to this story, is the equivalent of Realism, a view which allows those who espouse it to feel both that they are in the vanguard and that they are upholding essential English values.

The opposite but equally misleading view is the one taken by certain artists in particular, that there is nothing of any interest in the arts before Duchamp. Thus the American artist Joseph Kossuth claims that 'As far as art is concerned, Van Gogh's paintings aren't worth any more than his palette is', and that 'all art (after Duchamp) is conceptual (in nature) because art only exists conceptually'.

Parallel to this is the view of the critic who is only interested in the art of the past to the degree that in it are to be found hints of the Modernism to come, a view that even so intelligent a critic as Barthes at times comes dangerously close to espousing.

Despite such extreme claims as those of Kossuth, the fact remains that it is in the domain of art rather than literature and music that the most interesting and sophisticated explorations of Modernism are to be found, as my quotes from Joseph Koerner, Rosalind Krauss and Thierry de Duve in the course of this book demonstrate. I think this has to do with the fact that literature is too embroiled with the world while music can only properly be discussed by those with the technical know-how; painting, on the other hand, is 'purer' than literature, so that one can see more clearly what is at stake in painterly choices, while being, in principle at any rate, accessible for anyone to comment on.

The most powerful exponent of the purist view of Modernism was the New York art critic Clement Greenberg in the middle years of the twentieth century. 'I identify Modernism', he wrote,

> with the intensification, almost the exacerbation, of this self-critical tendency, that began with ... Kant ... The essence of Modernism lies, as I see it, in the use of the characteristic methods of the discipline to criticize the discipline itself – not in order to subvert it, but to entrench it more firmly in its area of competence.

Thus art is seen as searching for its essence, for that which is only art and nothing else – for all else is frippery, 'mere' convention. In this story all art is seen as moving towards abstraction, and then finally to Abstract Expressionism, New York style, as inevitably as history moves towards the dictatorship of the proletariat. The trouble with this is that it is deeply puritanical, and behaves towards the past rather as Mary Douglas accused Protestantism of behaving towards sacred history: it certainly has a vision of history, but it is a thin and selective one. Here, for example, is Greenberg on Mondrian: 'His pictures ... are no longer windows in the wall but islands radiating clarity, harmony and grandeur – passion mastered and cooled, a difficult struggle resolved, unity imposed on diversity. Space outside them is transformed by their presence.' This says something about Mondrian and helps us look at his pictures. It does so largely by means of a stark contrast between his pictures and all those that preceded them: they were windows let into the wall; his are islands of purity placed *on* the wall. That, in a way, is beautifully put, and illuminating (it occurs in a moving obituary of the painter). But after a while we start to ask: Are all pictures before Mondrian 'windows'? And, even if they are, are not the differences between them, between the windows of Leonardo and Rembrandt, say, or those of Vermeer and Cézanne, more important than the fact that they are all 'windows', that all of them ask us to look at some form of representation of the world isolated within the frame? Perhaps the answer is no, but Greenberg would have to do a lot more work to persuade us.

Thierry de Duve's book on Duchamp and Modernism, from which I have had occasion to quote, is similarly absolute, though more sophisticated. He brings out well how Duchamp's art as it evolved in the second decade of the twentieth century was aimed at subverting the pretensions of the pioneers of abstraction, especially Kandinsky, as much as the prejudices of the traditionalists. He quotes a lyrical passage from Kandinsky's *Reminiscences*, which ends: 'And then comes the imperious brush, conquering [the canvas] gradually first here, then there, employing all its native energy, like a European colonist who with axe, spade, hammer, saw, penetrates the virgin jungle where no human foot has trod, bending it to conform to his will.' And he comments:

> The text presents the tube of paint, then the palette, next the virgin canvas, and finally the brush, not as the tools of the painter . . . but as metonyms of potential yet accomplished paintings. But the tube of paint, the palette, the canvas and the brush are also the protagonists of an erotic saga which the rest of the text then unfurls, with dubious lyricism infused with machismo and colonialism.

De Duve rightly contrasts this with Duchamp's sending up of the colonialist enterprise in scattered remarks throughout his life, which he compares to that of Raymond Roussel in *Impressions d'Afrique*, but which could also be compared to Apollinaire's magnificent *Les Mamelles de Tirésias*. 'For Kandinsky's abstract expressionism, for Malevich's suprematism, for Mondrian's neoplasticism and for all the purisms that sprang between 1912 and 1914 from the idea of pure colour,' he goes on, 'Duchamp substituted eroticism, which, as he very seriously explained to Pierre Cabanne, he wanted to turn into a new artistic "ism".' There is, however, nothing very macho about Duchamp's eroticism, as we have seen, since the poor Bachelors never get to the Bride and have to be satisfied with what Duchamp, commenting on his chocolate-grinding machine, termed 'olfactory masturbation'.

De Duve uses Duchamp to throw doubt upon the enterprise of Kandinsky, Malevich and Mondrian, but also upon that of a later idealist like Beuys, whom he rightly sees as dreaming, like Novalis, of an ideal world replacing the real one. But of course he also uses Duchamp to throw doubt upon the whole notion of a tradition which, unaware that its foundations have been sapped, goes on acting as if it were imbued with authority, the authority to say what art is good and what art is bad; the authority to award prizes and to decide what art will be in and what out; the authority, finally, to decide what is art and what is not (is a bicycle wheel art? an enamel urinal?). Yet de Duve is no Duchamp. He does not quite know when to keep his mouth shut or how to speak only in riddles. With his back to the wall, so to speak, he is as prescriptive as Greenberg: 'When push comes to shove', he admits towards the end of his long book, 'Rodchenko is an artist and Bonnard is not.'

A painter friend of mine tells how, when he was a student at the Slade in the mid-1960s, Greenberg's was the view of art history with which they were confronted: Modernism went from Manet to Pollock via Cézanne, Cubism and abstraction. This explained everything that needed explaining in the eyes of the tutors, but it left no room for twentieth-century artists who interested my friend, such as Bonnard, Balthus, Beckman and Bacon, to stick only to the Bs. A decade or two later the scene was so dominated by Duchamp that the story would be very different: it would go from Seurat to Duchamp to Pop Art to all the varieties of conceptual art now being practised. There would still be no room for the four Bs. The question is: how to tell a story compelling enough yet supple enough to contain both Mondrian and Bonnard, both Schoenberg and Satie, both Kafka and Queneau?

One recent critic who has managed to do just that, it seems to me, is T.J. Clark in his magnificent *Farewell to an Idea: Episodes*

from a History of Modernism. Clark rightly recognises that modernity is bound up with disenchantment, which is linked to secu-
larism. He quotes Hegel in the *Aesthetics*: 'Art, considered in light
of its highest vocation, is and remains for us a thing of the past.'
This does not of course mean that art ceases after 1820, only that
its ability effortlessly to articulate the world has gone. Viewing
Modernism through the prism of Hegel's chapter on the Unhappy
Consciousness in the *Phenomenology*, he argues that for art to
remain meaningful in these changed circumstances it has to accept
what he calls contingency, and I have called arbitrariness. Art's
being able to continue, he argues, has depended on its being able
to make Hegel's dictum in the *Asesthetics* 'specific and punctual'.
'That is to say, on fixing the moment of art's last flowering at
some point in the comparatively recent past, and discovering that
enough remains from this finale for a work of ironic or melancholy
or decadent continuation to seem possible nonetheless.' This he
calls, invoking Beckett, the 'can't go on, will go on' syndrome. And
he understands that once the Hegelian view is accepted technique
will always be seen as 'a kind of shame', while at the same time
artists, desperate for something stable beneath their feet, will tend,
like Flaubert, to fetishize the notion of the sheer hard practical and
technical work involved in making art.

One of the great strengths of Clark's book is that he understands
(as I perhaps have been slow to do here) that even if there is a single
story of Modernism it cannot be told in purely linear fashion –
hence his subtitle. Writing about *episodes* in *a* history of Modernism,
he is free to explore a whole web of stories rather than trace any
linear sequence, and thus to restore a sense of history as being made
– by artists, by events – rather than simply lived out, that the blind
alleys down which artists have gone at certain periods of their lives
are as important as their achieved successes, and that different
responses are called for in pre-First World War France, in post-
Revolutionary Russia and in America after the Second World War.

Though I have borrowed the notion of the false friends of
Modernism from him to describe those who purport to be its
champions but who in fact distort and mislead, I have applied it
to a different group of people. For Clark the false friends are
those like Greenberg and Herbert Read who, in the 1950s, were
Modernism's most passionate advocates.

Even at the time it was chilling to see Greenberg's views become an orthodoxy. What was deadly, above all, was the picture of artistic continuity and self-sufficiency built into so much modernist writing: the idea that modern art could be studied as a passing-on of the same old artistic flame (. . .) from Manet to Monet to Seurat to Matisse to Miró . . .

He would have found a parallel in literary studies during that same period, though rarely articulated with the passion and elegance of Greenberg and Read. There Eliot, Proust and Virginia Woolf were co-opted into an essentially Christian discourse which stressed the redeeming powers of art and so, in like manner, blunted the anguish and often despair of these writers, and thus distorted their achievement. Today such readings seem not merely inadequate, but quaint. On the other hand, as I have suggested, Modernism is never short of false friends, whether in the guise of fervent American deconstructionists or coolheaded English poets and novelists.

One of the great strengths of Clark's book is the intensity with which he questions the art he is dealing with: *it matters*. As a result his book is full of brilliant *aperçus*. Two that chimed particularly with my own explorations here are, first, his comparison at one point of Pissarro's *Two Young Peasant Women* of 1892 with the exactly contemporary popular painting by Jules Breton, *June*. The latter presents us with an idealised scene of country folk at rest for us to gaze at in comfort: this is June in the countryside as we would like to imagine it. In contrast, in the Pissarro 'we could worry endlessly about the peasants' actual poses, and the distance between them, and where the ground plane is; but of course the painting does not offer us sufficient clues to answer these kinds of questions, and does not mean to. It means us to be in limbo. We have to come in close – too close to get the whole picture.' This is precisely the kind of contrast I was trying to establish between Némirovsky's treatment of the events of May 1940 and Claude Simon's. The difference is that no-one today would make any claim for Jules Breton but Némirovsky is compared to Tolstoy.

The second passage that struck a particular chord with me was Clark's discussion of what Picasso was up to in the summer of 1910 at Cadaqués. Picasso felt that the work he did in that period was a failure, not, Clark suggests, because he didn't get very far in his explorations, but because he got too far:

> Picasso was the last person to want, or perhaps to see how, to pursue the Cadaqués solution to its logical conclusion (Mondrian being the first). Therefore he changed course. He made his way back to the world of phenomena. He put together a great counterfeit of everything that had, at Cadaqués, evaporated under his brush.

I have followed Krauss in seeing the moment in which Picasso looked into the abyss of abstraction and then drew back as coming two years later, in the autumn of 1912, but the precise moment is not important, and the fact that Clark comes to the problem from so very different a starting point only reinforces my feeling that the shape of the argument is essentially correct and, again, can be applied across the arts: I suggested that Robbe-Grillet, faced with a similar moment, slipped over into the world of abstraction (which was also, for him as for Duchamp and his friends in 1913, the world of both commercial assembly-line production and of pop).

Where I part company with Clark is in his nostalgia for an art that will be both accepting of its contingency and yet public. That is why David means so much to him, and the work that Malevich and Lissitzky did together in Vitebsk in the early years of the Russian Revolution. That is why Cubism, that joint venture of Picasso and Braque, is seen by him as one of the heroic moments of Modernism. It is to this idea that he, invoking Wallace Stevens in his title, bids a reluctant farewell. Though rightly suspicious of the danger of being 'dazzled by old men musing on the days of their youth', he quotes what Picasso is reputed to have said to Françoise Gilot about those years and how they came to an end: 'As soon as we saw that the collective adventure was a lost cause, each one of us had to find an individual adventure. And the individual adventure always goes back to the one which is the archetype of our times: that is, van Gogh's – an essentially solitary and tragic adventure.'

Clark is profoundly suspicious, in what sometimes seems to me a very Marxist way and sometimes a very English way (let us say an English Marxist way), of what Walter Benjamin called 'aura', the resonance of a work of art or a fragment of the world at a particular moment, for each of us. He calls it 'coquetting with the unknowable', while Julian Barnes would call it 'believing in baa-lambs and hedgerow-blossoms and human goodness'. Not for them Wordsworth's 'deep inland murmur' or Proust's sudden access of joy at eating the madeleine or feeling the uneven paving-stones beneath his feet. My own temperament and background being different, I am deeply moved by those passages. I think of Modernism as that paradox, a tradition of those who have no tradition. And it does not seem to me that this is wholly tragic. Merleau-Ponty's reflections on Cézanne and Francis Bacon's remarks to David Sylvester help point the way: neither illustra-tion nor abstraction but the daily struggle of a dialogue with the world, without any assurance that what one will produce will have value because there is nothing *already there* against which to test it, but with the possibility always present that something new, something genuine, something surprising, will emerge.

And here Rosalind Krauss's explorations of Picasso and pastiche become seminal. Her argument, if I understand it correctly (for she likes to play with possibilities rather than committing herself to a viewpoint, feeling, rightly, that too often to pin down is to distort), is this: Adorno, in his *Philosophy of Modern Music*, so presented his case that Schoenberg was seen as the necessary culmination of a century of musical striving, while Stravinsky, his great rival, was seen as having sold out to fashion and bourgeois comfort in the years immediately following the First World War, with the inven-tion of a 'classicism' which merely plundered the past, magpie fashion, for whatever would suit his current needs, producing in the process music that was superficially attractive but was in the end merely opportunist. In the same way, Krauss suggests, John Berger makes the case against Picasso, arguing that when, after the war, his art no longer reflected social conditions, it lost itself in a flurry of brilliantly executed pastiches. In both cases, interestingly, Cocteau is the social butterfly who, in real life, leads the artist to betray his calling. But, asks Krauss, what if pastiche were not something modern art could simply eradicate in an access of purity but its dark shadow, the trap into which it was and is always likely to fall if it is to remain true to its calling? It is the purists like Adorno and Berger who have got it wrong, she implies; we cannot simply slice through Modernism in this way; each artist, each work even, must be judged separately and in its own terms, within the larger story of which each is a part. This means that argument and disagreement will never end, which is as it should be. I may feel that Chagall grew soft and vacuous after fifteen or so glorious years, but others may disagree. Our disagreement will have in the end to recognise what we each of us take the story of Modernism and even the story of art, or perhaps even the story of the world, to be, but none of these entities is fixed. They could always persuade me or I them, or further reading or viewing will persuade me, that I need to rethink. Randall Jarrell, in a famous essay on Wallace Stevens's *Collected Poems*, recounted how, when Stevens was publishing the great poems of his late middle years, *Notes Toward a Supreme Fiction* and *An Ordinary Evening in New Haven*, he, Jarrell, had taken him to task for becoming verbose and over self-conscious, but that now, with the evidence of the late poems before him, he had to admit that those miraculous works would never have come into being had it not been for the poetry of the middle years. In other words, the poet knew best, even if what he knew was hidden even from himself. The same may be true of Hockney; only time will tell. But of course that does not mean that the critic who admired the early Hockney should not lament what he sees, at present, as the taking of too many wrong turns, even if in the end he has to eat his words. And what does 'in the end' mean here? Even death may not bring an end to debate. Mallarmé can talk of eternity changing Poe into the being he always, essentially, was, but how we evaluate Poe (or Bacon or Stockhausen) will never be resolved once and for all. Donne remained an interesting minor poet till Eliot showed us how to read him.

There cannot, then, be a definitive 'story' of Modernism. We cannot step outside it, much as we would like to, and pronounce with authority on it. We can only try to persuade people to see it from our point of view. And we all have a *parti pris*. It was because Eliot was groping for a certain sort of poetry himself that he championed Donne in place of Milton; because Boulez composes a certain sort of music that he champions Debussy and Varèse (and Mallarmé); because my friend seeks to paint certain kinds of paintings that he wishes to fight for Bonnard and Beckman. A tradition is a living thing, and each major artist, as Eliot understood, leads to its reconfiguration, however minutely.

Krauss's admirable openness in relation to Picasso does not appear to extend to other modern artists. Her exploration of just why Picasso resisted abstraction, which seems to suggest that she sympathises with him, takes on a different colouring when seen in the context of her other critical writing on Modernism, which is concerned mainly with abstraction and photography, and appears to have little time for artists who have struggled to remain at the crossroads of figuration and abstraction, such as Bonnard or Bacon. My own 'story', as I have tried to present it here, discovering what it was as I went along, is that only an art which recognises the pitfalls inherent in both realism and abstraction will be really alive. That is why I warm to the novels of Perec and Bernhard more than to *Finnegans Wake* or the novels of Updike and Roth, to the pictures of Bacon and early Hockney more than to Pollock or Tracey Emin, to the music of Birtwistle and Kurtág more than to Cage or Shostakovitch.

But I realise that this may be largely because of who and what I am. The late R.B. Kitaj compared Cézanne's rootedness in his native Provence to what he called the 'diasporist' (horrible term) imagination of the uprooted Picasso, and he suggested that at some deep level Modernism and the diasporist imagination go together. This may be true if we have a flexible enough notion of diaspora to accept that an apparently rooted Frenchman like Bonnard or Englishwoman like Virginia Woolf could also have created a 'diasporic' art – and then one would want to look at Bonnard's relocation to the South of France in the latter part of his life as a kind of exile into which he went with his problematic wife, and at Virginia Woolf's sense of herself as a woman excluded from a male-dominated society. To that extent the Marxist critique of Modernism I mentioned at the start may have a point: Modernism may not be a consequence of the crisis of the bourgeoisie but it may be the product of a general European rootlessness in the wake of the French and Industrial revolutions. All will then depend on whether we see such rootlessness as pathological or as giving those who are imbued with it a certain vantage point, allowing them to see things which might otherwise have remained hidden. In other words, are we to see our own history, that which makes us what we are, as something which blinkers us or which sharpens our vision? This is, in itself, of course, a very Modernist question.

Notes

page 1, 'I feel I'm . . .' *Stéphane Mallarmé, Correspondance*, ed. Henri Mondor and Lloyd James Austin, Gallimard, Paris, 1965, vol. I, 1862–71, pp.150–1.
'My condition is this . . .' Hugo von Hofmannsthal, *The Lord Chandos Letter*, tr. and with a preface by Michael Hofmann, Penguin Books, Harmondsworth, 1995, p.9.
page 2, 'Everything fell into pieces . . .' *ibid.*, p.11.
'I hoped to cure myself . . .' *ibid.*, pp.11–12.
'For it is something . . .' *ibid.*, pp.12–13.
page 3, 'I lead a life . . .' *ibid.*, pp.17–20.
'towards the end . . .' *The Diaries of Franz Kafka, 1910–1923*, ed. Max Brod, Penguin, Harmondsworth, 1964, p.62 (3 October 1911).
page 4, 'I can't write . . .' Franz Kafka, *Letters to Friends, Family, and Editors*, tr. Richard and Clara Winston, John Calder, London, 1978, p.70 (15 December 1910; modified).
'During last night's insomnia . . .' *ibid.*, p.333 (5 July 1922; modified).
'I speak of an art . . .' Samuel Beckett, *Proust and Three Dialogues with Georges Duthuit*, Calder and Boyars, London, 1965, p.103.
page 5, Peter Gay, *Modernism: The Lure of Heresy*, William Heinemann, London, 2007.
page 6, 'Señor Picasso's painting . . .' *The Letters of Evelyn Waugh*, ed. Mark Amory, Penguin, Harmondsworth, 1980, p.214.
'all these cheerless creeps . . .' *The Letters of Kingsley Amis*, ed. Zachary Leader, HarperCollins, London, 2000, p.295.
page 12, 'Despite the studiously agnostic . . .' Alexandra Walsham, 'The Reformation and the "disenchantment of the world" revisited', *The Historical Journal*, Cambridge, June 2008, p.408.
Eamon Duffy . . . : see in particular *The Stripping of the Altars: Traditional Religion in England 1400–1580*, Yale University Press, New Haven, CT and London, 1994.
if not downright lies . . . : by philosophers from Wittgenstein and Heidegger to Foucault and Derrida, by anthropologists from Lévi-Strauss to Mary Douglas, by critics from Benjamin to Barthes – indeed, there is scarcely a major thinker of the past hundred years who has not had a go at unpicking the Protestant and Humanist myths.
cultural analysts such as Erich Heller . . . : Erich Heller, *The Disinherited Mind*, Penguin, Harmondsworth, 1961; Hans-Georg Gadamer, *Truth and*

Method (1960), English tr., Continuum, New York, 1975; Hans Blumenberg, *The Legitimacy of the Modern Age* (1966), English tr. MIT, Cambridge, MA, 1985; a lone English voice is Owen Barfield, *Poetic Diction: a study in meaning*, London, 1928.

page 13, 'Trust in the eternal laws . . .' G.W.F. Hegel, *Phenomenology of Spirit*, tr. A.V. Miller, Oxford University Press, 1977, p.455.

the key Romantic concern . . . : almost every serious writer on the topic has tackled the issue. Among the most illuminating discussions I have come across are two fairly old books, Geoffrey Hartman, *The Unmediated Vision*, Yale University Press, New Haven, CT, 1956, and Walter Jackson Bate, *The Burden of the Past and the English Poet*, Chatto and Windus, London, 1971.

page 14, Heller even . . . once . . . : 'The Hazard of Modern Poetry', a series of radio broadcasts printed in *The Listener* and subsequently reprinted with *The Disinherited Mind*. The passage is on pp.228–30.

page 15, The idea that there was a middle state . . . : Diarmaid McCulloch, *Reformation: Europe's House Divided 1490–1700*, Penguin, London, 2004, p.11.

page 17, *The Lamentation of Doctor Faustus*: Thomas Mann, *Doctor Faustus*, tr. A.D. Lowe-Porter, Penguin, Harmondsworth, 1968, p.466.

page 18, Even Frank Kermode . . . : *The Romantic Image*, Routledge and Kegan Paul, London, 1957, ch.8.

page 19, 'I realize that I shall be taken . . .' *Farewell to an Idea*, Yale University Press, New Haven, CT and London, 1999, p.409, n.10.

page 22, In his splendid book . . . : Erwin Panofsky, *The Life and Art of Albrecht Dürer*, Princeton University Press, 1955, p.156.

'As for geometry . . .' *ibid.*, p.171.

'The lie is in our understanding . . .' *ibid.*

page 23, 'I was unable to find . . .' von Hofmannsthal, *op.cit.*, pp.11–12.

page 26, 'Why must I think . . .' Mann, *op.cit.*, p.143.

page 27, 'Shall we see . . .' Rabelais, *Gargantua and Pantagruel*, tr. Sir Thomas Urquhart and Peter le Motteux, Oxford University Press, 1934, vol. I, p.98.

page 28, 'Idle reader . . .' Miguel de Cervantes, *Don Quixote*, tr. Edith Grossman, Secker & Warburg, London, 2004, p.3.

page 29, 'I picked up my pen . . .' *ibid.*, p.4.

page 30, 'Somewhere in La Mancha . . .' *ibid.*, pp.19–20.

page 31, 'so convinced in his imagination . . .' *ibid.*, p.21.

page 32, 'having given a name . . .' *ibid.*, p.23.

As Marthe Robert points out . . . : *L'Ancien et le nouveau: De don Quichotte à Franz Kafka*, Payot, Paris, 1963, p.138ff.

The standard view of the novel . . . : Adam Thirlwell, *Miss Herbert*, Jonathan Cape, London, 2007, pp.68–70.

one of the first episodes . . . : *Don Quixote*, Part I, chs iv and xxxi.

page 33, 'the juxtaposition of chivalrously good intentions . . .' Thirlwell, *op.cit.*, p.70.

page 35, 'Don Quixote was charging . . .' *Don Quixote*, tr. Edith Grossman, *op.cit.* p.64.

'In part one of this history . . .' *ibid.*, p.65.

page 36, 'in this account . . .' *ibid.*, pp.68–9.

page 37, 'is not, like the Homeric bard . . .' Robert, *op.cit.*, p.112–13.

'What differentiates the novel . . .' 'The Story-teller', in *Illuminations*, tr. Harry Zohn, Jonathan Cape, London, 1970, pp.87–8.

page 40, 'Among the eminent persons . . .' 'Napoleon; Or, the Man of the World', in *Selected Essays*, ed. Larzer Ziff, Penguin, Harmondsworth, 1982, p.337.
'In the plenitude . . .' *ibid.*, p.344.
page 42, In a wonderful passage . . . Mann, *op.cit.*, p.185.
page 44, 'whereas anxiety . . .' *The Concept of Anxiety*, ed. and tr. Reidar Thomte with Albert B. Anderson, Princeton University Press, 1980, p.42.
'anxiety is the dizziness . . .' *ibid.*, p.61.
page 45, 'a self that has no possibility . . .' *The Sickness Unto Death*, tr. Alastair Hannay, Penguin, Harmondsworth, 2004, p.65.
page 46, 'for without possibility . . .' *ibid.*, p.69.
'It is a psychological master-stroke . . .' *ibid.*, pp.139, 143.
page 47, 'What is masterly . . .' *ibid.*, p.143.
'If one wants to compare . . .' *ibid.*, p.68.
page 49, Dr Johnson's criticism of Milton . . . : 'Life of Milton', in *The Works of Samuel Johnson*, G. Walker, London, 1820, vol. XI, p.152.
Geoffrey Hartman has noted . . . : 'Wordsworth, Inscriptions and Romantic Nature Poetry', in *Beyond Formalism: Literary Essays 1958–70*, Yale University Press, New Haven, CT and London, 1970, pp.206, 224.
'each picture . . .' Joseph Leo Koerner, *Caspar David Friedrich and the Subject of Landscape*, Yale University Press, New Haven, CT and London, 1990, p.9.
page 50, 'Before Friedrich . . .' *ibid.*, p.13.
A good example . . .: For all Wordsworth's poetry and prose I use the one-volume Oxford edition, *The Poetical Works of Wordsworth*, ed. Thomas Hutchinson, revised by Ernest de Selincourt, in the 1959 reprint. Since I give the titles or (when there is none) the first line in the body of the text I dispense with page references here.
page 58, 'For it is something . . .' von Hofmannsthal, *op.cit.*, p.10.
page 60, *'Wanderer Above the Sea of Fog . . .'* Koerner, *op.cit.*, p.187.
page 62, 'In the framed nothingness . . .' *ibid.*, p.96.
page 66, Isaiah Berlin once called Verdi . . . : 'The *"Naïveté"* of Verdi', in *Against the Grain: Essays in the History of Ideas*, ed. Henry Hardy, Pimlico, London, 1997, pp.287–95.
I think John Bayley puts . . . : '*Oliver Twist*: "Things As They Really Are"', in John Gross and Gabriel Pearson (eds), *Dickens and the Twentieth Century*, Routledge & Kegan Paul, London, 1962, partly reprinted in *Charles Dickens*, ed. Stephen Wall, Penguin Critical Anthologies, Harmondsworth, 1970. The quotes are on pp.442–3 of this book.
page 67, 'One evening . . .' Søren Kierkegaard, *On Authority and Revelation*, tr. Walter Lowrie, Harper & Row, New York, 1966, p.69
page 68, 'For it is one thing . . .' *ibid.*, pp.3–4.
page 69, 'Among the so-called negative thinkers . . .' *Concluding Unscientific Postscript*, tr. David F. Swenson and Walter Lowrie, Princeton University Press, 1968, p.78.
page 70, 'Are you fond of . . .' Charles Dickens, *Oliver Twist*, ed. Philip Horne, Penguin, London, 2003, p.90.
page 71, 'When your brother . . .' *ibid.*, p.412.
'The Elector called out . . .' 'Michael Kohlhaas', in *The Marquise of O – and Other Stories*, tr. Martin Greenberg, Criterion, New York, 1960, p.182.

page 73, 'Never can dreams . . .' *Dreamtigers*, tr. Mildred Boyer and Harold Morland, Souvenir, London, 1973, p.24. The poem is on page 70.

Hamm in Beckett's *Endgame* . . . : Samuel Beckett, *Endgame*, Faber, London, 1958, pp.35–7.

page 74, 'Actuality cannot be conceived . . .' *Papers and Journals: A Selection*, tr. Alastair Hannay, Penguin, Harmondsworth, 1966, p.470.

'But it's not dead . . .' Samuel Beckett, 'Dante and the Lobster', in *More Pricks than Kicks*, Calder & Boyars, London, 1974.

page 77, 'Is a new beginning . . .' T.S. Eliot, *Four Quartets*, 'East Coker', Part V in *The Complete Poems and Plays* Faber, London, 1970.

page 78, 'The invaluable works . . .' Wordsworth, *op.cit.*, p.735. The whole passage is worth re-reading with Kierkegaard's comments in mind.

'Then he meets . . .' J.D. Salinger, *The Catcher in the Rye*, Penguin, Harmondsworth, 1977, p.125.

page 79, 'Is that what illustration . . .' David Sylvester, *Interviews with Francis Bacon*, Thames and Hudson, London, 1975, pp.99–100. The other quotations in this paragraph are on pp.17 and 63–4.

page 80, 'that cruel tense . . .' 'Journées de lecture', in *Contre Sainte-Beuve*, ed. Pierre Clarac and Yves Sandre, Pléiade, Paris, 1971, p.170.

'Through its *passé simple* . . .' Roland Barthes, *Le Degré zéro de l'écriture*, Seuil, Paris, 1953, pp.30–1.

page 81, quoted by André Breton . . . : *Manifeste du Surréalisme* (1924), in André Breton, *Manifestes du Surréalisme*, Gallimard, Paris, 1972, p.18. The passage runs: '. . . Paul Valéry qui, naguère, à propos des romans, m'assurait qu'en ce qui le concerne, il se refuserait toujours à écrire: *La marquise sortit à cinq heures*'.

page 82, 'The way old Freddie . . .' P.G. Wodehouse, *Young Men in Spats*, Penguin, Harmondsworth, 1971, p.8.

In Borges' story . . . : in Jorge Luis Borges, *Labyrinths*, ed. Donald A. Yates and James E. Irby, New York, 1964, pp.76–87

page 84, In 'The Garden of Forking Paths' . . . : *ibid.*, pp.19–29.

In 'Tlön, Uqbar, Orbis Tertius' . . . : *ibid.*, pp.3–18.

Borges' most famous story . . . : *ibid.*, pp.36–44.

page 86, Malcolm Bowie . . . : *Mallarmé and the Art of Being Difficult*, Cambridge, 1978, p.8.

Anthony Hartley provides this plain prose translation in his *The Penguin Book of French Verse: The Nineteenth Century*, Harmondsworth, 1957, p.197: 'The virginal, living, and beautiful day, will it tear for us with a blow of its drunken wing this hard, forgotten lake haunted beneath the frost by the transparent glacier of flights that have not flown? A swan of long ago remembers that it is he, magnificent but freeing himself without hope, for not having sung the country to live in, when the tedium of sterile winter shone. His whole neck will shake off this white agony inflicted by space on the bird that denies it, but not the horror of the earth where his feathers are caught. A phantom condemned to this place by his pure brilliance, he stays motionless in the cold dream of scorn worn in his useless exile by the Swan.'

page 87, 'with panic-stricken rapidity . . .' Bowie, *op.cit.*, p.9.

'The double effort . . .' *ibid.*, p.8.

'O the mind . . .' Sonnet, 'No worst, there is none', in *The Poems of Gerard Manley Hopkins*, ed. Robert Bridges, Oxford, 1956, pp.106–7.

page 88, 'The space created by the poem . . .' Bowie, *op.cit.*, p.144.

page 89, 'Tout se passe . . .' Preface to *Un Coup de dés, Oeuvres complètes*, ed. Henri Mondor and G. Jean-Aubry, Pléiade, Paris, 1945, p.455.

'Quite often the anecdotal . . .' 'Le Tour d'écrou', in *Le Livre à venir*, Gallimard, Paris, 1959, p.163.

page 92, 'This poem . . .' quoted in Bowie, *op.cit.*, p.125.

page 93, 'he chooses to depict . . .' Maurice Merleau-Ponty, *The World of Perception*, tr. Oliver Davis, London, 2008, p.40.

page 94, 'When our gaze . . .' *ibid.*, pp.40–1.

'a universe for the first time bereft . . .' Claude Simon, *La Corde raide*, Sagittaire, Paris, 1947, p.117.

page 95, 'to see the earth again', Wallace Stevens, 'Angel Surrounded by Paysans', in *The Collected Poems of Wallace Stevens*, Knopf, New York, 1954.

'These almost asexual bodies . . .' Simon, *op.cit.*, pp.115–16.

'It is Cézanne's genius . . .' 'Le Doute de Cézanne', in *Sens et non-sens*, Nagel, Paris, 1963, p.25. I use the translation in Galen A. Johnson and Michael B. Smith, *The Merleau-Ponty Aesthetics Reader: Philosophy and Painting*, Evanston, IL, 1993.

page 96, 'We live in the midst . . .' *ibid.*, p.28.

page 97, 'The painter recaptures . . .' *ibid.*, p.30.

page 98, 'Le calme. Le gris . . .' Robert Pinget, *Passacaille*, Minuit, Paris, 1969. An English version might run:

Calm. Greyness. Nothing moves. Something must be broken in the mechanism but nothing shows. The clock is on the mantelpiece, the hands tell the time.

Someone in the cold room would have just come in, the house was closed, it was winter.

Greyness. Calm. Would have sat down at the table. Numb with cold, till the fading of the light.

It was winter, the garden dead, the yard bare. No-one there for months, everything is in order.

The road that leads to the house skirts empty fields. Crows fly up, or magpies, visibility is bad, night is about to fall.

The clock on the mantelpiece is encased in black marble, the face rimmed in gold, roman numerals.

The man sitting at the table a few hours earlier found dead on the dung-heap would not have been alone, a sentry was on guard, a trusty peasant who had noted only the deceased on a grey day, cold, would have approached the slit of the shutters and seen him clearly dismantling the clock then remaining prostrate in his chair, elbows on the table, head in hands.

How to trust this murmur, the ear is not up to it.

page 100, 'The double effort required . . .' See above, note to *page 87*.

page 101, 'For centuries painters had faced . . .' Gay, *op.cit.*, p.155.

page 102, 'At first they seem . . .' Rosalind E. Krauss, *The Picasso Papers*, Farrar, Strauss and Giroux, New York, 1998, p.25.

page 103, 'The news items accumulate . . .' *ibid.*, p.39

'One of the fragments . . .' *ibid.*, p.27.

page 105, 'It is their unequal size . . .' *ibid.*, p.33

page 106, Every thought, he says . . . *ibid.*, p.46.

One way of doing this . . . *ibid.*, p.44.

page 107, A beautiful essay by John Mepham . . . : 'Figures of Desire: Narration and Fiction in *To the Lighthouse*', in G.D. Josipovici (ed.), *The Modern English Novel*, Open Books, London, 1976.

page 109, 'Building a modern imperial capital . . .' Robert Gildea, *Children of the Revolution: The French 1799–1914*, Allen Lane, London, 2008, p.83.

page 110, Marguerite Duras . . . : *L'Amante anglaise*, Gallimard, Paris, 1967.

page 114, 'Fernande has left . . .' Krauss, *op.cit.*, p.84.

'The avant-garde had moved on . . .' *ibid.*, p.127.

[Picasso] clearly loathed . . . : *ibid.*, p.126.

page 115, 'It is the historical logic of modernism . . .', *ibid.*, p.241.

page 116, 'The word "art" . . .' quoted in Thierry de Duve, *Kant After Duchamp*, MIT, Cambridge, MA, 1996, pp.161–2.

page 117, the story of *Fountain* . . . : I follow de Duve, *op.cit.*, pp.89–143.

page 119, 'if you analyze it, you will see . . .' Sylvester, *op.cit.*, pp.58–60.

page 121, let us remember Joseph Koerner's comments . . . : see above, note to *page 62*.

page 124, In a famous debate . . . : at one of the Cerisy *colloques*, see *Nouveau roman: hier, aujourd'hui*, Paris, 1972, vol. II, pp.51–2.

page *126*, as Kafka once said . . . : Max Brod, *Franz Kafka, A Life* (1937), Schocken Books, New York, 1959, p.75.

page 128, as Elizabeth Sewell showed . . . : *The Field of Nonsense*, Chatto & Windus, London, 1952.

page 131, 'We have a new advocate . . .' 'The New Advocate', tr. Willa and Edwin Muir, in Franz Kafka, *Collected Stories*, ed. Gabriel Josipovici, Everyman's Library, London, 1993, p.163 (I have altered the translation here and there to make the meaning clearer).

page 132, 'From Munich on . . .' quoted in de Duve, *op.cit.*, p.175.

page 133, Thierry de Duve suggests . . . : *ibid.*, pp.184ff.

page 135, For years he had been trying . . . : I have written a novel about the whole episode: Gabriel Josipovici, *The Big Glass*, Carcanet, Manchester, 1991.

page 136, In an interview . . . : quoted in Yve-Alain Bois, *Painting as Model*, MIT, Cambridge, MA, 1993, p.287.

'The whole scaffolding . . .' Mann, *op.cit.*, p.142.

'I speak of an art . . .' see above, note to page 73.

'If you really want to hear', Salinger, *op.cit.*, p.1.

page 137, 'They poked into the straw . . .' 'A Hunger Artist', tr. Willa and Edwin Muir, in Kafka, *op.cit.*, pp.231–2.

page 138, 'Dear Stieglitz . . .' quoted in de Duve, *op.cit.*, p.140.

page 139, 'They who have been accustomed . . .' Wordsworth, *op.cit.*, p.734.

page 140, Evelyn Waugh's response . . . : see above, note to page 6.

'The essential argument . . .' Bois, *op.cit.*, p.180.

page 141, 'The broad-backed hippopotamus . . .' 'The Hippopotamus', in Eliot, *op.cit.* See Hugh Kenner, *The Invisible Poet*, W.H. Allen, London, 1960, pp.72–80, for some fine remarks on Eliot's quatrain poems of 1917–22.

Or as when Queneau . . . : *Zazie dans le métro*, Gallimard, Paris, 1959, p.7.

page 142, 'Certain events would put me into a position . . .' *On Certainty*, tr. Denis Paul and G.E.M. Anscombe, Blackwell, Oxford, 1979.

page 145, 'the peculiarity of ancient tragedy . . .' Søren Kierkegaard, *Either/Or*, vol. I, tr. David F. Swenson and Lillian Marvin Swenson, Doubleday, New York, 1959, p.141.

'The chorus', says Kierkegaard . . . : *ibid.*

page 146, 'The reason for this . . .' *ibid.*
'Our age has lost . . .' *ibid.*, p.147.
'Where the age loses the tragic . . .' *ibid.*, p.143.
'In ancient tragedy . . .' *ibid.*, p.141.
page 147, 'The truth is . . .' John Jones, *On Aristotle and Greek Tragedy,*
Chatto & Windus, London, 1962, p.14.
'Aristotle's treatise begins . . .' *ibid.*, p.29.
page 148, 'to our sense of characteristic conduct . . .' *ibid.*, p.33.
'Masking . . . flourishes . . .' *ibid.*, pp.44–5.
The *oikos* consists . . . : *ibid.*, pp.82ff.
page 149, 'When he says that Klytemnestra . . .' *ibid.*, p.117.
'The Necessity that crushes . . .' *ibid.*, p.129.
page 150, 'No question of Sophocles' superiority . . .' *ibid.*, p.148.
'All men . . . are teleologically blind . . .' *ibid.*, p.168.
'In both Aeschylus and Sophocles . . .' *ibid.*, pp.170–4.
His objective pollution . . . : *ibid.*, p.232.
page 151, 'What renders innocent . . .' *ibid.*, p.234.
page 153, 'When Orestes saw . . .' *ibid.*, p.272.
'Clearly defined terminal climax . . .' *ibid.*, p.266.
page 154, 'but the two marshallers of the host . . .' I have deliberately chosen
A.T. Murray's rather archaic-sounding translation (Loeb Classical Library,
London, 1928) because it seems to me to capture what must already have felt
archaic to Homer's first audience in a way no smart up-to-date translation
ever can.
page 157, 'The red creature . . .' *The Inheritors,* Faber, London, 1961, p.216.
page 159, 'Instead of making an objective . . .' quoted in de Duve, *op.cit.*
As Leo Steinberg has shown . . . : 'The Algerian Women and Picasso at
Large', in *Other Criteria,* Oxford University Press, New York, 1972,
pp.125–234.
page 160, '*Pulcinella* was my discovery of the past . . .' Igor Stravinsky and
Robert Craft, *Expositions and Developments,* Faber Music, London, 1962,
pp.113–14.
page 163, 'He spoke sententiously . . .' Anthony Powell, *At Lady Molly's,*
Heinemann, London, 1957, p.55.
'If it had not been such an intolerably hot evening . . .' Angus Wilson,
Hemlock and After, Penguin, Harmondsworth, p.87.
' "Jake," said Madge . . .' Iris Murdoch, *Under the Net,* Penguin,
Harmondsworth, 1960, p.178.
page 165, ' "What is it, Mary?" . . .' Ian McEwan, *The Comfort of Strangers,*
Jonathan Cape, London, 1982, p.85.
'She had always seen decay . . .' V.S. Naipaul, *Guerrillas,* Penguin,
Harmondsworth, 1976, p.55.
'We had by now descended . . .' Philip Roth, *The Ghost Writer,* Penguin,
Harmondsworth, 1980, p.79.
Barthes pointed out . . . : in *Mythologies,* tr. Annette Lavers, London,
1973, p.95.
page 168, 'In the Péricand household . . .' Irène Némirovsky, *Suite Française,*
tr. Sandra Smith, Chatto & Windus, London, 2006, p.6.
page 169, ' "This is a disaster" . . .' *ibid.*, p.85.
'. . . on this road . . .', *La Route des Flandres,* Minuit, Paris, 1960, pp.14–17.
The French reads:

... sur cette route qui était quelque chose comme un coupe-gorge, c'est-à-dire pas la guerre mais le meurtre, un endroit où l'on vous assassinait sans qu'on ait le temps de faire ouf, les types tranquillement installés comme au forain derrière une haie ou un buisson et prenant tout leur temps pour vous ajuster, le vrai casse-pipe en somme ... ce qui ne l'empêchait pas de se tenir toujours droit et raide sur sa selle aussi droit et aussi raide que s'il avait été en train de défiler à la revue du quatorze juillet et non pas en pleine retraite ou plutôt débâcle ou plutôt désastre au milieu de cette espèce de décomposition de tout comme si non pas une armée mais le monde lui-même tout entier et non pas seulement dans sa réalité physique mais encore dans la représentation que peut s'en faire l'esprit (mais peut-être était-ce aussi le manque de sommeil, le fait que depuis dix jours nous n'avions pratiquement pas dormi, sinon à cheval) ... deux ou trois fois quelqu'un lui cria de ne pas continuer (combien je ne sais, ni qui ils étaient: j'imagine, des blessés, ou cachés dans des maisons ou dans le fossé, ou peut-être de ces civils qui s'obstinaient de façon incompréhensible à errer traînant une valise crevée ou poussant devant eux de ces voiturettes d'enfant chargées de vagues bagages (et même pas des bagages: des choses, et probablement inutiles: simplement sans doute pour ne pas errer les mains vides, avoir l'impression l'illusion d'emporter avec soi, de posséder n'importe quoi pourvu que s'y attachât – à l'oreiller éventré au parapluie ou à la photographie en couleurs des grand-parents – la notion arbitraire de prix, de trésor) comme si ce qui comptait c'était de marcher, que ce fût dans une direction ou une autre ...)

page 171, I have already ... : see above, note to page 32.
He quotes Flaubert ... : Thirlwell, *op.cit.*, p.47.
'be true to the mess ...' *ibid.*, p.47.
page 172, 'The most radical novels ...' *ibid.*, p.426.
as David Daiches once pointed out ... : personal communication.
as when Dickens ... : *The Pickwick Papers*, ed. Mark Wormald, Penguin, London, 1999, pp.130–1; *A La Recherche du temps perdu*, Pléiade, Paris, 1987, vol. I, p.318.
what Clement Greenberg once said ... : 'Towards a Newer Laocöon', in *Clement Greenberg: The Collected Essays and Criticism*, ed. John O'Brian, 4 vols, Chicago, 1986, vol. I, p.27.
page 173, 'The problem of living in Brazil ...' Thirlwell, *op.cit.*, p.378.
page 174, 'I was an idealistic adolescent' Julian Barnes, *Nothing to be Frightened of*, Jonathan Cape, London, 2008, p.32.
' "I hope, Barnes ..." ' *ibid.*, p.170.
page 175, 'Like most Victorian novelists ...' Bayley, *op.cit.*, p.451.
As Linda Colley ... : *Britons: Forging the Nation 1707–1837*, Yale University Press, New Haven, CT and London, 1992.
page 176, 'In his delightful novel ...' Malcolm Bradbury, *Rates of Exchange*, Secker & Warburg, London, 1983, p.152.
page 178, the American artist Joseph Kossuth ... : 'Art after Philosophy', quoted in de Duve, *op.cit.*, p.300.
page 179, 'I identify Modernism ...' 'Modernist painting', in *The New Art*, ed. Gregory Battcock, Dutton, New York, 1973, p.66.
rather as Mary Douglas ... : *Natural Symbols*, Penguin, Harmondsworth, 1973, pp.40–1.

'His pictures . . . are no longer . . .' obituary of Mondrian, reprinted in Greenberg, *Collected Essays* vol. I, pp.188–9.

page 180, 'The text presents . . .' de Duve, *op cit.*, pp.158–9.

'For Kandinsky's abstract expressionism . . .' *ibid.*, p.159.

page 181 'When push comes to shove . . .' *ibid.*, p.432.

page 182, He quotes Hegel . . . : Clark, *op.cit.*, p.371.

'That is to say . . .' *ibid.*

'a kind of shame' *ibid.*, p.48.

page 183, 'Even at the time . . .' *ibid.*, p.175.

'we could worry . . .' *ibid.*, p.87.

page 186, 'Picasso was the last person to want . . .' *ibid.*, p.192.

'As soon as we saw . . .' *ibid.*, p.222.

page 186, Randall Jarrell, in a famous essay . . . : 'The Collected Poems of Wallace Stevens', in Randall Jarrell, *The Third Book of Criticism*, Farrar, New York, 1965.

page 187, The late R.B. Kitaj . . . : *First Diasporist Manifesto*, Thames and Hudson, London, 1989.

Index

Page numbers in italics refer to figures.

Acknowledgements

Thanks first of all to Naomi Segal, director of the Institute for Advanced Studies, University of London, for inviting me to give the lecture which was the germ for the present book, and to Alan Jenkins at the *Times Literary Supplement* for encouraging me to provide him with a shortened version of it, and for many discussions of the nature and implications of Modernism over the years. Thanks, too, to George Craig for reading a draft of my lecture with his usual meticulousness and critical acumen, but even more for forty years of stimulating conversation about every aspect of literature from Rabelais to Beckett. Rosalind Belben read the completed typescript with a writer's eye and a care which, though I have to a certain extent grown used to it over the years, never fails to fill me with wonder. Stephen Mitchelmore, Julian Bell, Jeremy Lane and Timothy Hyman also read the script and were generous with their comments, criticism and encouragement. With all of them this was but a stage in a conversation about art and about Modernism which has been going on for a very long time, and which, as Sancho Panza says, will never be done. They have saved me from many errors and gently suggested ways in which the book could be improved. And Michael Wood, at a late stage, professed enthusiasm for the project while harbouring grave reservations about some portions of the typescript. As a result of his criticism I hope I have produced a better book. To all of them I am profoundly grateful. Last but not least, Tamar Miller kept me from taking myself too seriously while never doubting the seriousness of the enterprise.

For permission to reprint copyright material the author and publishers gratefully acknowledge the following: Random House, Inc. and Faber and Faber Ltd for lines from *The Collected Poems of Wallace Stevens* (1954); Faber and Faber Ltd for lines from *The Complete Poems and Plays of T.S. Eliot* (1970); Chatto & Windus for extracts from *On Aristototle and Greek Tragedy* (1962) by John Jones; Farrar Straus and Giroux for extracts from *The Picasso Papers* (1998) by Rosalind E. Krauss; Harvill Secker for lines from Cervantes' *Don Quixote* translated by Edith Grossman (2004).